epistemology

First Books in Philosophy

Blackwell's *First Books in Philosophy* series presents short, self-contained volumes which together provide a comprehensive introduction to the field. Each volume covers the major issues relevant to the subject at hand (e.g., philosophy of religion, ethics, philosophy of literature), and gives an account of the most plausible attempts to deal with the problems at hand.

Epistemology *Richard Fumerton*

Forthcoming:

Feminist Philosophy *Claudia Card*
Historical Introduction to Ethics *John Hare*
Philosophy of Religion *Edward Wierenga*
Modern Philosophy *Keith Yandell*

epistemology

richard fumerton

Blackwell
Publishing

BLACKWELL PUBLISHING
350 Main Street, Malden, MA 02148-5020, USA
9600 Garsington Road, Oxford OX4 2DQ, UK
550 Swanston Street, Carlton, Victoria 3053, Australia

The right of Richard Fumerton to be identified as the Author of this Work has been asserted in accordance with the UK Copyright, Designs, and Patents Act 1988.

First published 2006 by Blackwell Publishing Ltd

1   2006

Library of Congress Cataloging-in-Publication Data

Fumerton, Richard A., 1949–
    Epistemology / Richard Fumerton.
       p. cm. — (First books in philosophy)
    Includes bibliographical references and index.
    ISBN-13: 978-1-4051-2566-6 (hardcover : alk. paper)
    ISBN-10: 1-4051-2566-7 (hardcover : alk. paper)
    ISBN-13: 978-1-4051-2567-3 (pbk. : alk. paper)
    ISBN-10: 1-4051-2567-5 (pbk. : alk. paper)   1. Knowledge, Theory of.
    I. Title.   II. Series.

    BD161.F855 2005
    121—dc22

                                                        2005009253

A catalogue record for this title is available from the British Library.

Set in 10 on 12.5 pt Galliard
by SNP Best-set Typesetter Ltd., Hong Kong
Printed and bound in India
by Replika Press Ltd

The publisher's policy is to use permanent paper from mills that operate a sustainable forestry policy, and which has been manufactured from pulp processed using acid-free and elementary chlorine-free practices. Furthermore, the publisher ensures that the text paper and cover board used have met acceptable environmental accreditation standards.

For further information on
Blackwell Publishing, visit our website:
www.blackwellpublishing.com

For Maureen and Michael
and all you have done for Mom and Dad

Contents

Preface

You are on a jury. Your task is to decide whether the evidence shows that it is beyond reasonable doubt that Jones murdered his wife. One bit of evidence you might be tempted to weigh heavily is that in the majority of cases crimes of this sort are committed by people very close to the victim. But at the same time you feel a bit uneasy about reaching a conclusion about a *particular* person, Jones, based on merely statistical evidence of this sort. On the other hand, it seems that evidence you *are* supposed to take very seriously might be, on analysis, equally statistical. Mary, an eyewitness testifying for the prosecution, claims to have seen Jones driving his white Toyota near the scene of the crime. But recent studies suggest that despite the faith we place in eyewitness testimony (as opposed to, for example, circumstantial evidence), such testimony is often very unreliable. In any event, it certainly isn't 100 percent reliable, so if we do trust an eyewitness we are presumably doing so based on statistical facts about the frequency with which eyewitnesses of this sort get matters right. Also, forensic evidence concerning blood type found near the scene of the crime, DNA, and the like, all clearly bear on the question of whether it is likely that Jones murdered his wife, but only statistically. So it better be possible to reach conclusions about particular individuals based on statistical facts if we are to reach any conclusions about individuals at all. Now for you to reach a rational conclusion about some matter to which somebody testifies, for example, must you have independent *justification* for believing that the testimony is reliable, or is it enough that the testimony *is* reliable and that you are forming beliefs based on that testimony in a way that is, in this case at least, likely to lead to truth?

Change the example slightly and imagine *yourself* a witness in a trial. You thought you saw Jones in his car near the crime scene. The defense lawyer begins to question you and informs you of studies that indicate that eyewitness testimony is not nearly as reliable as one might have supposed. After presenting such evidence the lawyer asks you again if you are reasonably certain that it was Jones driving the car. If rational, should you now begin to wonder whether or not you were right? If the studies can weaken your justification for believing what you did, would it also be true that your failure to have any independent reason for trusting the "evidence of your senses" in such situations should itself weaken, or perhaps even destroy, any evidence you might have thought you had? More generally, for *any* way you have of reaching conclusions, should we suppose that such conclusions are only rational insofar as you have good reason for thinking that that way of reaching conclusions is reliable? But if we require *that* much for rational belief in a conclusion, might we not be in serious trouble? On the assumption that one can't use a method of arriving at the truth to justify our belief that that very method is reliable (without begging the question), won't the requirement that we certify all of our ways of forming beliefs inevitably lead to failure? After all, we can't evaluate *all* of our ways of forming beliefs without using at least one of those methods.

In this book we'll try to examine more carefully some of the issues touched upon above. Epistemology can certainly seem to have a fundamental place in philosophy. It is not clear that one can be interested in philosophy, or for that matter interested in *truth*, without being interested in epistemology. Any claim made in philosophy, any controversial and interesting claim made in *any* context, inevitably invites an epistemological question. When you make a controversial assertion to an intellectually curious person, that person will want to know how you know the truth of what you claim. That person will want to know what your evidence, if any, in support of the claim is. To evaluate, at least in an ideal way, claims about knowledge and evidence, it is tempting to suppose that one should have a firm grasp of what knowledge and evidence are, of how one can come to know or rationally believe an assertion.

In what follows, I'll try to presuppose as little philosophical knowledge as possible. I want this book to be accessible to those without any formal training in philosophy. At the same time, I don't want to sacrifice clarity, precision, and philosophical sophistication for accessibility. As a result, I hope the book will be of interest not only to the novice but also to the seasoned philosopher. But the demands of accessibility have forced me to make difficult decisions, particularly when it comes to omitting discussion of important and interesting arguments and views. And adherents of certain views may occasionally wince at the way in which their positions are painted with very broad strokes. I have tried to focus on arguments for and against certain kinds of views that do not depend on the often subtle, interesting and valuable distinctions among those views. I have also tried to be as evenhanded as I can between radically different approaches to epistemology. The most interesting controversy in epistemology today is that raging between the internalists and externalists. While I won't try to hide my own philosophical views, I do try very hard to be fair to those with whom I disagree. Indeed, it is much more important to me that the reader understand the reasons both internalists and externalists have for advancing their views than that the reader ends up sharing my views.

I conclude each chapter of the book with a short list of suggested readings. Some are well-known and highly influential. Others are less well-known, but are chapters of books or articles that I have found particularly clear, accessible, and helpful.

I'd like to thank Mike Mulnix for his help in editing an early draft of this manuscript. I'd also like to express my appreciation to Deborah Heikes for her helpful comments and criticisms. I owe a very special debt of gratitude to Mike Huemer and Tim McGrew who spent an enormous amount of time and energy providing extensive and detailed suggestions for improving an earlier draft of the manuscript. They tried valiantly to save me from myself and, I hope, often succeeded. The book is much better for their invaluable advice. I also thank the University of Iowa for providing me the developmental leave during which most of the book was written.

Chapter 1

Introduction

The Subject Matter of Epistemology

Epistemological questions involve the concepts of knowledge, evidence, reasons for believing, justification, probability, what one ought to believe, and any other concepts that can only be understood through one or more of the above. This first claim, like most others in philosophy, is controversial. Not all epistemologists would include, for example, justification as a paradigmatic epistemological concept. And in any event, we need to restrict much further the interpretations of terms and phrases like "know," "justification," "reasons for believing," and "what one ought to believe" if we are to locate the primary focus of the epistemologist's interests. Before getting immersed in heated controversies, we might be able to make some preliminary and relatively uncontroversial helpful distinctions.

Consider, for example, the concept of knowledge. We use the term "know" in a variety of ways. We talk about knowing how to do certain things (how to play tennis, how to swim, how to golf). We also talk about people and places we know (I know Richard Foley and Paris). But of most interest to the epistemologist are claims to have *propositional* knowledge – knowledge *that* things are so and so (e.g. that space is finite, that there is a God, that there is a mind distinct from matter). The knowledge is called propositional because the "that" clause that takes the object of the verb "knows" expresses a proposition, something that is either true or false – it is either true or false that space is finite and that there is a God.[1] But why should the philosopher interested in knowledge focus on propositional knowledge?

1

It is at least initially tempting to suppose that the concept of propositional knowledge is more fundamental than knowing how or knowing people and places. One might suppose, for example, that to know how to play golf is just to know certain truths – that one will hit the ball farther if one keeps one's left arm straight, that consistency requires keeping one's head down, and so on. Similarly, one might suppose that knowing a city reduces to knowing a great many truths about the city – the location of streets, landmarks, buildings, etc. Neither view is terribly plausible, however. Dogs know how to swim, but it's unlikely they know any truths describing their activities. I had a good friend determined to improve his golf game and who acquired endless propositional knowledge in that pursuit. His ability to play golf diminished in direct proportion to his acquisition of propositional knowledge. And it seems at least possible that someone could be very familiar with a city, and in that sense know it, even though that same person gets confused very easily and would be extremely hard pressed to describe in any informative way that very city.

In any event, there is a simpler answer to the question of why philosophers are most concerned with propositional knowledge. As philosophers we are most interested in getting at the *truth* about various matters. And the epistemological questions that so interest us are those that are the immediate and natural challenges raised by the intellectually curious in response to assertions. If you tell me confidently that there is a God, or that the CIA assassinated Kennedy, I'll want to know how you know that that is so. I'll want some reasons or justification for believing that it is true. I'll want to know why you think that this is something a rational person ought to believe. It's this fact about our pursuit of truth that makes plausible the claim that one simply cannot ignore epistemology and pursue other philosophical investigations. Philosophers respond to virtually all controversial claims with requests for evidence or justification, and that leaves the philosopher uninterested in epistemology in a precarious position indeed.

So it is the interest in truth that leads us inevitably to propositional knowledge. It remains an interesting question as to what conceptual connections exist between, for example, knowing how, and knowing that. It is surely not a coincidence that the same term is used in describing both capacities (knowing how) and propositional knowledge (knowing that). It also remains to be seen whether even after restricting our attention to propositional knowledge we can uncover some *univocal* understanding of that in which we are interested.

If preliminary distinctions are useful before discussing knowledge, they are also critical to the list of other candidates for concepts that concern the epistemologist. Consider, for example, the idea of having a reason to believe some assertion. Talk of reasons for believing is ambiguous at least between (1) causes of belief, (2) epistemic reasons for belief, and (3) pragmatic, moral, and conceivably even legal reasons for belief. Putting forth reasons for belief comes most naturally in response to "Why" questions. One might, for example, ask why Sam believes that God exists. One way of distinguishing different senses of "reason for believing" is to think about quite different sorts of answers one could give to the question. One might, for example, answer the question by pointing to the fact that Sam was raised in a very religious community by parents who conditioned Sam to believe in God at a very early age. The answer is perfectly appropriate if we are interested in identifying the causes of Sam's belief – if we are interested in causal reasons. But the epistemologist is not interested in the causes of belief, except in a sense that I shall argue shortly is of only marginal interest.

Some would argue that it is also possible to treat belief as an action and that one can have reasons for believing analogous to the reasons one has for acting in a certain way. Suppose you want some milk to pour over your cereal and you know that the corner store sells milk. That might give you a reason to walk to the corner store. The reason seems to have something to do with the fact that the action in question would accomplish, is likely to accomplish, or at least might accomplish some goal or end. Such reasons are sometimes thought of as pragmatic. Believing seems also to be the sort of thing that could accomplish some goal or end of the believer. Pascal famously argued that we have good reason to believe in God insofar as there is a chance that such belief will enable us to avoid eternal damnation. He seemed to argue that to have such a reason it need not even be all that likely that the goal or end would be accomplished. Given the stakes, a reasonable person would attempt to protect himself from the overwhelmingly disastrous possibility that there are horrors a God has in store for a non-believer. Someone paralyzed by fear of death might have powerful reason to attempt to bring about belief in an afterlife, a belief that might allow a more effective pursuit of happiness in this life.

It is by no means obvious that one *can* legitimately treat believing as an action for which one can have pragmatic reasons. Some have claimed that one can have pragmatic reasons only for that which is in some sense under our voluntary control. One can't *decide* to believe something, the argument goes, the way one can decide to play a round of golf. Still, almost all agree that one can do things to increase the likelihood of having a belief, and for our present purposes we need only note that if there can be pragmatic reasons for believing some proposition, they are not the kinds of reasons that concern an epistemologist.

Just as there might be pragmatic reasons for believing, so also there might be moral reasons for believing. Some would argue that a parent has a kind of duty (and hence a moral reason) to believe in a child's innocence, even in the face of some rather credible evidence that the child is guilty. One can even imagine a "1984" society in which the powers that be have legislated certain beliefs – have required by law, for example, that people believe in an egalitarian society. If we can make sense of legal requirements to have belief we can also make sense, perhaps, of having a legal reason to believe what one does. But again, neither moral nor legal reasons are the subject matter of epistemology.

The reasons that concern the epistemologist are reasons that, if good, are supposed to make probable (or at least increase the probability) of the proposition believed being true. And even here we must be careful. Believing that I'll recover from a horrible illness might increase the probability of my doing so, but only by causing (or contributing to a cause of) my getting well. If I have good epistemic reasons (I'll also sometimes refer to these epistemic reasons simply as epistemic justification) for believing that I'll get well, then those reasons (that justification) must make likely that I'll get well, where that relation is not reducible to one of causing my getting well. In offering "analyses" of such concepts as having an epistemic reason to believe, philosophers will want to generalize from examples like that just given. To do so, we use placeholders or *variables* for people and the propositions they believe, where the idea behind the placeholder is that you can substitute for it the name or description of any person or proposition you like. So the idea suggested above amounts to this: S (where "S" refers to any person you like) has epistemic reasons to believe a proposition P (where "P" refers to any proposition you like) when S has reasons that make likely the truth of P, and this relation of making likely is not reducible to causing or contributing to a cause of what makes the belief true. This first stab at explaining the difference between epistemic reasons and other sorts of reasons invokes the concept of probability, one of those concepts on our list of concepts that define the enterprise of epistemology. As we'll see later there is a great deal of controversy about just how to understand that critical concept.

I suggested above that epistemologists are also concerned with questions about what one ought to believe. The distinctions made above apply here as well. Arguably, we use "ought" judgments to describe the reasons (usually all things considered reasons) people have for acting or believing. But if we can distinguish pragmatic, moral or legal reasons from epistemic reasons, then we will need to distinguish questions about what one pragmatically, morally, or legally ought to believe, from questions about what one epistemically ought to believe. We'll need to remind ourselves of this obvious fact when we return later to questions concerning the so-called "normativity" of epistemic judgments.

In discussing different sorts of reasons there might be for believing a proposition (and corresponding truths about what "ought" to be believed), it is worth emphasizing that the different kinds of reasons one might have for a belief are not exclusive. The cause of a belief, for example, might be the possession of an epistemic reason for believing. Indeed, on some views in order for you to have an epistemically justified or rational belief, you must *base* your belief on the good epistemic reasons you possess, and this basing is itself understood causally. So, for example, as a juror you might possess extraordinarily good epistemic reasons for believing that the defendant is guilty, but if you base your belief that he is guilty on the fact that he has a tattoo – your belief is caused by the fact that you become aware of his having a tattoo – your belief might still be unjustified or irrational. Furthermore, many would argue that your belief's having this source undermines the possibility of your knowing your conclusion. Notice that in making this point we relied on a distinction between reasons in your possession and reasons that are effective in producing belief. Some philosophers mark this distinction by contrasting the fact that there are reasons for you to believe *P* with the fact that you believe *P* rationally. We'll talk more about this in discussing the concepts of epistemic justification and rationality.

Metaepistemology vs. Applied Epistemology

Let's suppose we have tentatively identified a list of concepts that figure in questions that at least partially identify the field of epistemology. There is yet another distinction that has been implicit in the history of epistemology but that has been defined more clearly in recent decades – the distinction between *metaepistemological* questions and *applied* epistemological questions. Applied epistemology is also sometimes referred to as normative epistemology, but for reasons I'll give in chapter 3, I worry about the use of "normative" in this context. We can make the distinction between metaepistemology and applied epistemology focusing primarily on knowledge, with the understanding that a similar distinction can be made with respect to other epistemic concepts.

There are two quite different sorts of questions I can ask about propositional knowledge. I can ask what we know, if anything, and how we know it. Or I can ask what knowledge is. I'm calling the first sort of question an applied epistemological question; the second, a metaepistemological question. Before the terminology was introduced in epistemology, an analogous distinction was commonplace in twentieth century ethics – there it was labeled the distinction between metaethics and applied ethics. Philosophers interested in metaethics want to know what such properties as being good and being right are, if indeed there are such properties at all.[2] And they justify their preoccupation with this question on the grounds that one is hardly in a position to argue about what is good or right, unless one first understands precisely what the subject matter of the debate is. Analogously, at least some epistemologists would argue that we better get very clear about just what knowledge or rational belief is before we start arguing about what we know or rationally believe. It's not that we are not interested in figuring out what we know – the claim is rather that we need to get clear about just what it is that we are talking about before we engage in the search for knowledge and rational belief.

The argument as just presented is a bit suspect. It is hardly the case, for example, that my electrician needs a philosophical account of causation before he is a position to discover the cause of my light's flickering. But as we'll see, some philosophers are bent on making trouble for those interested in claiming knowledge (justification, rational belief, etc.), and it is more plausible to suppose that to diagnose the efficacy of such efforts (or, at the very least, to guard against the tricks of a philosopher) one needs the philosophical sophistication that comes from having an adequate account of the concepts employed in the debate.

Applied epistemology

Perhaps the dominant figure in the history of epistemology is the skeptic. While skeptics often implicitly presuppose some account of knowledge or justification, their status as skeptics is defined in terms of claims they make about what we know, or more precisely don't know, or aren't justified in believing. That the skeptic has been such a pervasive and influential figure in philosophy is not surprising. Philosophers, by nature, tend not to take things at face value. To be sure, we seem to be quite confident that we know all sorts of things, or at least that we have good reason to believe some hypotheses rather than others. But a moment's reflection reminds us that people have been quite certain that they knew "truths" that turned out to be false. The history of science is littered with one discarded theory after another. An atheist, quite literally, would have trouble surviving in philosophy at certain historical moments. These days it is hard to find theists in the philosophical community. Just as our legal system is built on the presupposition that the best way to uncover the truth about guilt and innocence is to subject the question to the intense debate of trial, so also, philosophers tend to think that the best way to uncover the truth about any matter that interests us is to subject the matter to intense debate. The skeptic plays the role of prosecutor – many epistemologists think of themselves as the defenders of common sense.

There are interestingly different versions of skepticism. It's certainly critical to distinguish skeptics about knowledge from skeptics about rational belief. So, for example, I might think that we can't know that the "big bang" theory of the "origin" of the universe is correct, while I am nevertheless convinced that we have pretty good reason to suppose that it is. As the example indicates, we can also relativize skepticism to a subject matter. I might be a "knowledge" skeptic with respect to virtually all highly theoretical claims made by science but be perfectly sanguine about the prospects of knowing commonplace truths about the breadbox-sized objects I take to be before me under optimal conditions of perception. On one extreme end of the spectrum of skepticism concerning knowledge, there is the philosopher who claims that we don't, and perhaps can't, know truths of any sort. And the most extreme of skeptics claim that we don't have any epistemic reason to believe any proposition (including, presumably, the proposition stating their skepticism).

The kind of skepticism that has driven so much of epistemology is usually fairly dramatic. Indeed, while philosophers do seem to argue over applied epistemological issues, the issues they argue about tend to be odd sorts of questions. Do we know, or justifiably believe, and if so how, any propositions about the past, the future, the physical world, other minds, etc. In part this is just an instance of a more general feature of philosophy. Alston and Brandt (1967), in a once widely used introduction to philosophy, describe philosophical questions as those that "by reason of their ultimacy and or generality are not treated by any of the more special disciplines." It might have been better to suggest that philosophical questions are so fundamental that they are not even entertained by those in more specialized pursuits of knowledge. As you will soon see, philosophers don't agree about much of anything, and that includes characterizations of what they do for a living. But I'm sympathetic to the idea that an applied epistemological question becomes philosophical only when it addresses a kind of knowledge or justification that is presupposed in most ordinary contexts. While I would like very much to know whether financial experts know that the stock market is going up or down, I would-n't dream of trying to get such knowledge from philosophers (acting in their capacity as philosophers).

If we are interested in responding to the skeptic who makes the out-landish claim that a certain class of propositions can't be known (or even rationally believed), we will be forced in short order to evaluate a slew of metaepistemological controversies. Indeed, we will use the challenge of skepticism as a way of organizing much of our metaepistemological dis-cussion. As we'll see, the force of a skeptic's argument, and the way in which one might respond to the skeptic, will depend critically on one's understanding of epistemic concepts.

Metaepistemology

I have already suggested that we will inevitably be forced to discuss metaepistemological questions. But I have also been painfully vague in my characterization of metaepistemology. The metaepistemologist, I said, asks what knowledge (justification, rationality, evidence) is. But that ques-tion is understood by philosophers in radically different ways. The dispute over what we are doing when we ask such questions is *metaphilosophical* – it is a dispute in the philosophy of philosophy. And we are not going to settle it here. The most I can do is give you a feel for the sometimes quite radically different approaches one takes to answering questions of the form "What is knowledge?"

One sort of philosopher takes what is sometimes called a linguistic turn. The relevant question for that philosopher concerns the *meanings* of various terms. The most perspicuous form a metaepistemological ques-tion takes for that philosopher is the following: What do we mean when we say of some person that he knows or rationally believes some propo-sition *P*? The answer to the question takes the form of an analysis. And on one (though only one) conception of analysis one tries to break the meaning of a knowledge claim, say, down into component claims each of which captures part of what it means to say of someone that he knows, and all of which together exhaust the meaning of knowledge claims. Pro-ponents of this conception of philosophical analysis have almost always insisted that analysis not only may, but must end – ideally in the unana-lyzed or indefinable. There must be some terms the meanings of which we grasp and which we use in turn to explain the meanings of other terms.

The idea that analysis consists of breaking down the complex into its simple parts is not, however, restricted to those who conceive of the targets of their analysis as the meanings of terms. Other philosophers think that they are trying to break down concepts or ideas, properties, or facts into their simpler constituent concepts or ideas, properties or facts. On the property view, for example, when we say of someone that he knows that *P* we are attributing to that person some property which, if complex, is reducible to a collection of simpler properties (the way that being a square can be thought of as composed of being a quadrilateral, having equal sides, and having right angles). The proponents of meaning analysis, concept analysis, and *traditional* property and fact analysis have agreed that their enterprise is in some sense radically different from the scientific effort to discover the ultimate building blocks of reality (atoms, electrons, quarks, and the like) – the stuff out of which all other stuff is made. It is a bit tricky to understand meaning analysis in such a way that one can discover the meanings of terms from one's "armchair," but you might, perhaps, be able to restrict the primary object of your interest to the way in which you *yourself* use terms like "know" – a project that at least relieves you from the obligation of conducting extensive surveys. If one takes properties to be the objects of one's analysis, one might hold that the property is something that one can "hold before one's mind" as one performs one's philosophical dissection.

Broadly speaking, the philosophers discussed above share the idea that philosophy is an activity one can at the very least conduct from the armchair. They also share the idea that the results of their analyses should in some sense be *necessary* truths. In saying what knowledge is, we don't want to discover some property or properties of knowledge that it just happens to have. It may be, for example, that I have a God-like Uncle Fred who has infallible beliefs about who knows what. It might be true that something is known if and only if Fred believes that it is known. But that fact about knowledge – interesting though it may be – still tells us nothing about what knowledge is.

These days, matters are considerably more complicated. A great many philosophers (particularly those who endorse the naturalism we will discuss later) think that one should model one's attempt to discover the nature of knowledge (justification, evidence, or whatever) on the scientist's attempt to discover the nature of water (lightning, electromagnetic fields, or whatever). It is sometimes suggested that stuff like water forms a "natural kind." We pick the kind out by reference to relatively superficial characteristics of the stuff (its appearance and taste, for example), but when we get seriously interested in discovering what water is we search for its underlying structure. That underlying structure is supposed to be somehow more critical to something's being water than the appearances water presents. In the rather poetic language of some philosophers, water

9

has its molecular structure in all possible worlds, while its appearance could quite conceivably change from world to world.

It is far from clear that one can make sense of this notion of terms that pick out natural kinds by reference to non-essential features of instances of that kind (where a non-essential feature is a feature the thing has but could have lacked). But even if we were to grant the many controversial philosophical assumptions needed to support the intelligibility of such a view, to employ this conception of analysis in the pursuit of answers to metaepistemological questions, we would need some unproblematic way to pick out knowledge (rational belief, propositions that ought to be believed). As we shall soon see, in the context of philosophical debate *uncontroversial* examples of knowledge, or even rational belief, are hard to come by. The skeptic hovers over us prepared to charge us with begging important questions when we assume that we know this, that, or the other truth. In a number of important works Chisholm suggested that we need to decide at the outset whether or not we are going to take skepticism seriously.[3] His own view was that we should simply assume without argument that we have knowledge and rational belief and use our best examples of such knowledge and justified belief to guide us in constructing views about what knowledge or justified belief is. The problem, as we shall soon see, is that we seem very fond of views that are difficult to reconcile with a number of our most commonplace claims about what we know or have reason to believe.

I warned you that we were not about to settle metaphilosophical disputes concerning the nature of philosophy. As a result, we are not about to settle the more particular metaphilosophical disputes about the nature of metaepistemological questions. It might have been better not to bring the subject up. In fact, though, it is striking that philosophers with radically different understandings of what they are doing when they ask metaepistemological questions seem to have relatively little trouble engaging in the give and take of argument over the specific answers to those questions that have been proposed. When we join in the metaepistemological debate, I will most often employ the preferred language of those who think of analysis as meaning analysis. I suspect it will be possible for those with different views to find ways of translating the discussion into the terminology they prefer.

In what follows I am going to begin in chapter 2 with a discussion of what has historically been thought to be the most fundamental concept in epistemology, the concept of knowledge. As we shall see, the question of whether it deserves to have a fundamental place among epistemological concepts is a matter of some controversy. In chapter 3, we will turn

10

to our discussion of epistemic rationality, a concept that some take to be crucial to our understanding of knowledge. We will begin our discussion of epistemic rationality with an examination of certain structural questions that leave open the precise analysis of key concepts. There are dramatic differences among philosophers who share convictions about the structure of justification, and to those differences we will turn in chapters 4, 5, and 6. In chapters 4 and 5 we will focus on dramatically different accounts of what some call foundational justification. In chapter 6 we will examine inferential justification – justification that some claim rests on the kind of justification discussed in chapters 4 and 5. Finally, in chapter 7 we will see how the way in which one responds to skeptical challenges depends critically on the metaepistemological positions one adopts.

Suggested readings

Audi, Robert. 1998. *Epistemology*, Introduction. New York and London: Routledge.
Ayer, A. J. 1956. *The Problem of Knowledge*, chapter 1. New York: Penguin.

Notes

1 Even those philosophers who use the expression "proposition" disagree dramatically over just how to understand that to which the expression refers.
2 Such questions do not exhaust the subject matter of metaethics. Questions concerning knowledge of ethical truths, the connection between ethical concepts and other concepts, and the connection between moral conclusions and motives for acting, to take a few examples, also fall within the purview of metaethics.
3 As representative, see the first edition of Chisholm's *Theory of Knowledge*, chapter 4.

Chapter 2

The Analysis of Knowledge

When I began the last chapter with a list of concepts that concern epistemologists, there was a reason that the concept of knowledge headed the list. Philosophers have been obsessed with understanding and achieving propositional knowledge since Plato wondered in the *Theatetus* 2,500 years ago what must be added to true belief in order to get knowledge. In the history of epistemology before the twentieth century explicit reference to justification, reasons for believing, or probability was much rarer than it is today. Certainly, the primary focus was knowledge. But if knowledge is the paradigmatic subject of epistemological investigation, it is in many ways the most puzzling, and a number of philosophers, myself included, have decided that it should be of secondary interest to the epistemologist – that we should be more concerned with epistemic reasons for belief. But that decision certainly needs to be justified.

So what is supposed to be so puzzling about knowledge? Plato's search for a condition that must be added to true belief in order to get knowledge suggests that in order to know we must at the very least believe a true proposition. "Belief" might be too weak. Indeed, when we go out of our way to indicate that we merely believe a proposition, we are often trying to warn the person to whom we are talking that we lack knowledge. ("Do you know if the bus runs on Saturday?" I'm asked. "Well," I respond, "I *believe* that it does.") In any event, in at least some contexts, we seem to require something more like subjective *certainty* in order to have knowledge, where subjective certainty is a belief-like state (an absolutely firm conviction with no trace of doubt).

The so-called truth condition for knowledge seems relatively unproblematic. Knowledge is what some philosophers call a *factive* state. In the last chapter we noted that propositional knowledge is knowledge *that* something is the case. The noun clause following the verb expresses the propositional content of the knowledge state (conveys that which can be true or false). But we use noun clauses to complete any number of verbs describing psychological states. Someone S can know that P, believe that P, desire that P, hope that P, fear that P, be proud of the fact that P, regret that P, perceive that P, remember that P, and so on. Some of these descriptions of people can only be true if P is true. Others can be true whether or not P is true. If the description of the state can only be true if P is true, the state is factive. So, for example, we can believe that P, fear that P, desire that P, or hope that P whether or not P is the case. We can't know that P, it seems, unless P is true. In its most typical uses, we also can't perceive that P or remember that P unless P is true (though we can certainly seem to perceive or seem to remember that P when P isn't the case). Regret and pride are more difficult to characterize. It's not clear whether or not one can be truly described as regretting that one insulted a person if one didn't (though again one certainly can be in a "regret-like" state).

In an influential recent work, Williamson (2000) suggests that knowledge is the most *general* kind of factive state and that states like perceiving and remembering are species of knowledge – ways of knowing. Whether or not that is true, it does seem that as we ordinarily use locutions like "perceives that P" or "remembers that P" we can't truly describe people as perceiving that P or remembering that P unless they know that P. This, of course, doesn't entail that perceiving that, or remembering that are *species* of knowledge – they might instead be complex states that include knowing as a constituent. (The opening face-off is not a species of playing a hockey game, though it is a part of it.)

Whatever the connection is between knowledge and other factive states, the truth condition for knowledge seems relatively unproblematic. It certainly sounds *very* odd to suggest that someone can know that which is false. But it also seems that someone can be absolutely convinced of some proposition which is in fact true, even when that person doesn't know that truth. I might be wildly pessimistic and become certain that the plane I'm about to board will crash. If it does, I won't be able to comfort myself with a true parting thought that at least I checked out knowing well in advance of my demise. I might be wildly optimistic and become convinced that the lottery ticket I possess is destined to win. Should I happen to be right, we surely won't conclude that I really did know that I was about to win a fortune. So again we might naturally be led to Plato's question – What in addition to being sure of a truth do we need in order to possess knowledge?

The "Traditional" Analysis of Knowledge

It is an enormous understatement to suggest that philosophers have not exactly agreed on an approach to answering the question. A view often referred to as the "traditional" analysis of knowledge suggests that knowledge is true conviction coupled with good enough reason supporting the conviction. In the examples above, our pessimist and optimist had no knowledge because they had no good (epistemic) reason to believe what they did. Of course, if we try to explain knowledge by reference to epistemic reasons (or justification, or evidence, or what we ought to have believed, or what was likely) we will need an account of the critical epistemic concepts in terms of which we are trying to say something interesting about knowledge – and that account had better not presuppose an understanding of knowledge or we won't be making any headway. We can see already how philosophers who take this approach to understanding knowledge might think that the concepts in terms of which we explain knowledge are, trivially, conceptually more fundamental than the concept of knowledge – our understanding of knowledge is parasitic on our understanding of these other epistemic concepts.

In this chapter, we are going to try to operate as if we have some understanding of what it is to have reasons or justification or evidence in support of a belief. Relying on an intuitive understanding of these concepts, we can still make some common-sense distinctions. It seems as if reason, justification or evidence for believing is something that comes in degrees. I might have good reason to believe both P and Q, but have better reason to believe P than Q. In the language of probability, my epistemic situation might render P more probable than Q even if both are very likely to be true given all of the reasons in my possession. Again, on the supposition that we understand all this talk about reasons, evidence, and probability, we might wonder how much reason we need in support of our acceptance of P in order to know that P.

The Standards of Evidence and Knowledge

In attempting to answer that question, we might begin with the observation that in at least *some* contexts we seem to insist on very strong standards for knowledge – we require that our justification make what we believe overwhelmingly likely. Descartes famously seemed to suggest that in order to know some proposition P, our epistemic situation E would

14

need to be so good that it eliminated any possibility of error. Philosophers often use the abbreviation, $P(H/E) = n$, to refer to the fact that the probability of a given hypothesis H relative to evidence E is equal to a certain number, a number falling between 0 and 1, where 0 represents no chance, 0.1 represents a 10 percent probability, 0.2 represents a 20 percent probability and so on, until we get to 1, which represents 100 percent probability. So the Cartesian suggestion is that to know that H on the basis of evidence E, it must be the case that $P(H/E) = 1$.[1] And indeed the juxtaposition of a claim to know with the admission that there is a chance of error does sound very odd. "I know that the Yankees have won more world series than any other team, but they might not have," Fred says. That's a claim that produces cognitive dissonance – it grates on our attempt to understand the speaker. It is interesting to note, in this context, that jurors are only told that they need to find the defendant guilty beyond a reasonable doubt in order to convict. They are specifically *not* told that they must conclude that they *know* that the defendant is guilty in order to convict. And I suspect that the reason is precisely that if the instruction were put in terms of knowledge, it would be too difficult to get a conviction. Someone on the jury would always be able to point out that some wild hypothesis introduced by the defense could be true – has a chance of being true – and would thereby persuade at least some that they don't after all know (or perhaps know with certainty) the guilt of the defendant.

These days, Cartesian standards for knowledge are often dismissed with the quick observation that requiring justification *that* strong for knowledge would imply the absurd conclusion that virtually all of our knowledge claims are false. Whether that is true, as we shall see, depends a great deal on the interpretation of the relevant concept of impossibility in the locution "impossibility of error." At the moment, I am again relying on a kind of intuitive understanding of our talk about chance and probability. I said that a good deal of epistemology is shaped by the ever-present figure of the skeptic. Most epistemologists think of themselves as the defenders of common sense, where a commitment to common sense is often thought of as requiring that we find a way of preserving the truth of at least most of our everyday claims to have knowledge (or reasonable belief). If we require that in order to know our evidence must preclude the possibility of error, the fear is that we have surrendered too quickly the high ground in the battle with the skeptic.

It certainly does seem that we do claim to know all sorts of propositions, often with evidence far worse than that which Descartes sought. "Do you know what time it is?" I ask. "Yes," you respond, glancing at your wristwatch, "It's 5:00 p.m." But you surely are not in a position to eliminate the possibility that your watch isn't working correctly. You know that, and I know that, but neither of us raises a fuss about the knowledge claim. "Do you know where you'll be working next year?" I ask my son. "Yes," he replies, "I'll be working for Skadden in New York." We both know that the earth could be hit by an asteroid in the next few months, but that doesn't seem to constrain our knowledge claim. So obviously, if we presuppose that people are minimally rational and sincere in their knowledge claims, it is wildly implausible to suppose that they understand those claims as asserting the impossibility of error.

Puzzles Involving Closure

On the other hand, I have already suggested that there are contexts in which high probability of truth doesn't seem to be nearly enough for knowledge. In his book John Hawthorne (2003) builds a discussion of knowledge around data concerning what we take to be just obvious concerning what we can and can't say about knowledge of the outcome of fair lotteries. It is just a fact that virtually no one feels comfortable claiming to know that a ticket just bought in the lottery is a losing ticket. It might have only a one in a million chance of winning, or a one in a trillion chance of winning, but the fact that it has a chance at all seems to preclude legitimately claiming to know that it is a losing ticket. Consider another example borrowed from Hawthorne. If you are offered a million-dollar flight insurance policy for a dime, you will surely buy the policy. Why? Because you know that there is a chance that the flight will go down in flames – you certainly don't know for sure that it won't. If you did, you would be irrational to buy the policy and it obviously isn't irrational. But a moment before buying the policy, you might have casually claimed to know that you'd be staying at the Hilton in Paris for the next three days, though you were perhaps unsure where you'd be after that. But if you really did know that you'd be in Paris at all, let alone at the Hilton, you'd also know that you weren't going to be killed in a plane crash. At least this is so if knowledge is, in the technical language of epistemologists, *closed* under known entailment.

What is it for knowledge to be closed under known entailment? Claims about the closure of knowledge are best understood as claims about what other knowledge one is in a position to possess, given that one knows P and certain truths about what P entails. (For our purposes here, we can say that a given proposition P entails another Q when it is absolutely impossible that P be true while Q is false.) There is a great deal of recent discussion concerning so-called *closure* principles involving both knowledge and justified belief. Again, much of the discussion takes place in the shadow of skepticism. The following principle strikes a lot of us as about as obvious as a principle can be: If you know some truth P, and you know that P entails (guarantees the truth of) Q, then you are at least in a position to know Q. This is called *single* premise closure because the principle applies only to a known entailment from a single proposition. It also seems fairly plausible to embrace *multi-premise* closure – the idea that if you know that P and know that Q and that know that $(P$ and $Q)$ entails R, then you are in a position to know R. So in our example, if you know that you are going to make it to the Paris Hilton, and that proposition you know entails that you will make it through your transatlantic flight alive, then the single premise closure principle implies that you are in a position to know that you won't die on your flight. But then why are you taking out flight insurance?

In the lottery case, we can see how much trouble one would get in should one accept multi-premise closure and try to "bite the bullet" by claiming that we do after all know that the ticket just bought is a loser. If the high probability of its losing (when it does) allows us to know that it is a loser, and the high probability of each of the other losing tickets allowed us to know that they were losers, then there would be this very complicated conjunction of claims about losing tickets that we could know (the conjunction formed by a description of all but the winning ticket being losers). The conjunction, however, isn't even *likely* to be true – it has a very high probability of being false.

Notice that neither the lottery nor the flight example involve critically the fact that the proposition in question is a proposition about the future.[2] The lottery might already have been held (though the results are not now known by me) and my wife's flight might already have either crashed or landed when I'm offered the deal on life insurance for her flight. We still wouldn't feel comfortable claiming to know the fate of either the ticket or my wife.

So on the face of it, something has got to give. Either we don't know that we'll be in the Paris Hilton, or we do know that the flight won't crash, or there is something wrong with our closure principles. A number of epistemologists point the finger at closure principles. Such principles have often been viewed with suspicion because of the role they (often) sometimes play in the arguments of the feared skeptic. Descartes famously wondered how we could know that we are not living a vivid dream. These days it might be more effective to evoke *skeptical scenarios* (possible situations incompatible with our common-sense beliefs) employed in the plots of popular films like *Total Recall* or *The Matrix*. The idea presupposed in these films is that all of the subjective evidence we possess in support of commonplace beliefs about our physical environment are psychological states that are the immediate products of brain states. If we can manipulate (unbeknownst to the subject) the brain so as to produce the subjective appearance, we can produce precisely the same beliefs that result from veridical experience (experience of objects that are really there). The skeptic argues that once we consider these skeptical hypotheses carefully, we realize that we are simply in no position to rule them out – they are defined in such a way that they are perfectly compatible with all of the evidence we possess. But if we can't know that the skeptical hypotheses are false, and knowing that there is a table in front of me (when I know that its existence implies the falsehood of certain skeptical hypotheses) requires being in a position to rule out the skeptical hypotheses, then either we don't know that the table is there or there is something wrong with closure. As we shall see there are analyses of knowledge that would enable us to reject closure principles, but the closure principles are so intuitive that one should surely look with great suspicion on any view incompatible with them.

Contextualism

If the culprit isn't closure then we might reconsider ordinary knowledge claims. If we don't know that the flight won't crash and the reason is that there is obviously a chance that it will, then we need an explanation of why we are so promiscuous in our knowledge claims. Perhaps we consciously or unconsciously *exaggerate* when we make knowledge claims. Perhaps our knowledge claims are abbreviated versions of more complicated claims that we are willing to endorse. I'll talk about these possibilities shortly. But there is another idea that is becoming increasingly popular – a view called *contextualism*. The contextualist argues, in effect, that what a knowledge claim asserts varies from context to context – hence the name "contextualism." The view is usually introduced with analogies. Consider, for example, the adjective "tall." It seems relatively uncontroversial that we will call the very same person tall in one context who is described as short in another. Tall pygmies are very short NBA centers. There is no great paradox here once we reflect on the fact that judgments about height implicitly involve a reference class. Someone isn't tall or short *per se*. People are only tall or short relative to some class presupposed in the context of the claim (in comparison with some particular group of other people presupposed in the context of the claim). And there are all kinds of expressions like "tall." Flat mountain ranges are bumpy landing fields. Brilliant scientists can be stupid philosophers. So perhaps we should understand knowledge claims as always making implicit reference to some context of utterance.

Interestingly, there is a sense in which at least some contextualists want to pay lip service to the Cartesian idea that in order to know one must eliminate the possibility of error, at least in the sense that one must be in a position to eliminate all *relevant* alternatives to what one believes. If I claim to know that the butler committed the murder, I need to be in a position to eliminate the other suspects – this follows fairly directly from application of closure principles. The key difference in the contextualist's account of knowledge is the emphasis on *relevant* alternatives. According to the contextualist, what counts as a relevant alternative varies from context to context.

There are important variations on the basic idea of contextualism and one of these variations depends on whether the contextualist thinks that it is features of the person making the knowledge claim that determine which alternatives are relevant or whether it is features of the person about whom the knowledge claim is made that determine which alternatives are relevant. Philosophers who favor the latter sometimes prefer that their account not be called contextualist as they claim that there are set rules that all attributions of knowledge respect concerning subject-relative relevance – the relevance of context is built right into a meaning that doesn't shift from context to context. Though the differences between the two views are important, we needn't worry too much about them for the purposes of our present discussion. Whether we think that it is the speaker's or the subject's situation that determines whether an alternative is relevant, we are obviously going to need some instructions as to how to figure out when in a given context an alternative is relevant and needs to be eliminated by our evidence.

In an influential article, David Lewis (1996) suggests a number of speaker-relative criteria that determine when a given alternative is relevant. Put another way, he suggests various features of a person making a knowledge claim that determine when that person must be in a position to rule out a given alternative in order to make a true knowledge claim. One such rule, the rule of attention, states that when we actively *consider* a certain possibility, it automatically becomes for us in that context an alternative that we need to eliminate in order to make a true knowledge claim. Hawthorne suggests that we replace mere consideration of a proposition

19

with taking seriously the possibility. Either way, one can immediately see how in the context of a lottery or buying flight insurance, the ticket's winning or the flight's crashing are going to come to mind as real possibilities – the very concept of a lottery brings to mind the possibility of an unlikely fortuitous event occurring, and the very concept of insurance against disaster calls to mind the possibility of an unfortuitous, perhaps very unlikely, event occurring. Because in these situations I am seriously considering a possibility that I can't rule out, it would be inappropriate to make the relevant knowledge claims. In the context of odd philosophical discussions (of a sort we'll be engaging in throughout this book) we might be considering seriously some of the *skeptical* scenarios discussed above and that would explain how in those contexts we might become sympathetic with the skeptic's claim that we can't know ordinary truths about the world around us. When I give someone the time, however, neither of us might be paying any attention to the obviously very real possibility that my watch doesn't keep the right time, and when you asked if I knew what hotel I was staying in after my flight, I wasn't thinking about crashes, heart attacks, strokes, Armageddon, or for that matter, vivid dreams or *Matrix*-world mind manipulation.

The rule of attention by itself isn't going to do much work. People can be exceedingly stupid and fail to consider all sorts of possibilities that they *should* have considered. If I'm exceptionally pessimistic, I might be absolutely certain that the lottery ticket I was just given will be a loser, and I might not even consider as a live possibility that it isn't. Does anyone really want to claim that obstinacy helps achieve knowledge in the lottery case? Lewis himself notes (though only in passing) that one must always view as relevant those alternatives that *should* have been considered (whether they were or not) – he includes this in something he calls "the rule of belief" (the rule that any alternative believed to obtain automatically becomes relevant). Of course, that italized "should" is most naturally understood as the epistemic "should," and we seem to be back to square one. How low must the probability of an hypothesis be in order for it to be permissibly ignored in the context of evaluating a knowledge claim? And whatever level of probability we settle on, aren't we still going to be faced with the fact that we'll be forced to deny multi-premise closure? For each commonplace belief we form, alternatives to *its* truth might be exceedingly unlikely even though it is quite likely indeed that at least one of those beliefs has an alternative to it that is true.[3]

Another of Lewis's rules is the "rule of resemblance." It requires that we may never legitimately ignore an alternative that resembles in the right way a relevant possibility. This rule is supposed to help with the lottery puzzle in that the situation in which I win with a ticket is supposed to be relevantly like the situation in which I lose. One must wonder, however, what makes the winning situation relevantly like the losing situation. In one sense, the world in which I win is very different from the world in which I lose – when I win a lottery, I get very lucky, lucky in a way in which I rarely get lucky. If we count such unlikely worlds as relevantly like the world in which I lose the lottery, then why isn't the skeptic in business when he argues that dream worlds are relevantly like worlds in which we aren't dreaming? We'll return to the skeptic in some detail in chapter 7.

Fantl and McGrath (2002), Stanley (2003), and Hawthorne (2004) have all suggested that there might be a *pragmatic* dimension to the truth conditions for knowledge claims. Even when we have some pretty good evidence for the proposition, we are hesitant to claim that we know that an action will have a certain result, the argument goes, when a very great deal hinges on our being right. We are much more sanguine about making a knowledge claim even possessing mediocre evidence when we don't *care* all that much about being right. More generally, we are hesitant to claim to know a proposition if we are in a context in which we are not prepared to presuppose the truth of that proposition (to treat it *as if* it had a probability of 1) in making decisions. That might partially explain why we are relatively easygoing with respect to claims that people make about having had knowledge in the past. When your annoying friend bets on Crazylegs to win the fourth at Belmont, wins his bet, and brags that he just *knew* that the horse was a winner the moment he heard the name, you'll probably just let it go. When the contestant on the game show gets the right answer on the million-dollar question based on a vague feeling that it was correct, it is a bit churlish to raise questions about whether he really *knew* the answer after all. The view would also explain why in most contexts we don't challenge the knowledge someone claims to have about the time of day. On *most* occasions it doesn't matter all that much to us if we are given the wrong time. On the other hand, when we are considering the wisdom of flight insurance, we are obviously unprepared to treat the possibility of our flight crashing as zero. And when we buy a lottery ticket, we are hardly treating the possibility of winning as zero.

It is hard to see how pragmatic considerations can do much work in securing the truth of knowledge claims. The pragmatic contextualist wanted it to turn out that we do know most of the time what we are going to be doing tomorrow, the next day, next week and perhaps even this summer. But if we attempt to retain the closure principle (albeit relativized to contexts), it is still hard to see how one can reconcile our ordinary knowledge claims with our pragmatic situation. It is important to remember that we can be rational or irrational both for our actions and for our *failures* to act and while one gets a feel for the idea that in the context of buying life insurance one is not taking one's future as certain, the very considerations that argue for buying life insurance also argue for not getting rid of it once bought. Since I'm someone who does have life insurance and who is quite rational for not getting rid of it, now, five minutes from now, tomorrow or next week, it's hard to see how I am ever in a context in which I can treat my future existence as certain. But if that's so, then how can I claim to know where I'll be five minutes from now, tomorrow, or next week when if I were treating those claims as if they had a probability of 1, that would make irrational my failing to terminate my life insurance?

Error Theory and Knowledge Claims as Elliptical

Contextualists go through considerable gyrations trying to figure out a way to make most of our everyday knowledge claims turn out true. They are driven, understandably, by the undeniable fact that that we do make a great many knowledge claims, often without having overwhelmingly strong evidence supporting that which we claim to know. But it has always been my experience that it is just as obvious a datum that people are extremely quick to give up their knowledge claims when pressed. When you tell me the time and I ask if you know for sure, perhaps even mentioning the possibility of a broken clock, you'll probably just retract your knowledge claim. The contextualist will, no doubt, argue that I have changed the context by making vivid (and relevant) certain alternatives, but you are surely capable of answering a question about the correctness of your past knowledge claim – the claim you made before I changed the context. And it still seems pretty obvious to me that most people are quick to acknowledge that strictly speaking they didn't know – that what they said wasn't true. The view that the vast majority of ordinary knowledge claims are, strictly speaking, false, is one that should surely be taken seriously when the very people who make those claims don't seem willing to exert much energy defending them.

But what is going on? Are people just exaggerating when they claim to know things even though their evidence renders the propositions claimed to be known far less than certain? Should we construe their assertions as analogous to my wife's infamous "assertion" that she will be ready in a minute (where as best I can tell the minute referred to ranges anywhere from twenty minutes to an hour)? Years before contextualism gained popularity, Butchvarov (1970, part I) pointed out that we are often casual in making claims about knowledge that we realize are, strictly speaking, false. We describe various beliefs as knowledge knowing full well that they fall short of the ideal. Consider an analogy. When we are trying to teach our children the difference between various shapes, we'll draw a triangle-like figure, or a circle-like figure and describe the figures as triangles and circles respectively. The figures don't meet the formal geometrical definitions of triangles and circles (the lines aren't perfectly straight, or circular) and we know this. But the figures will do as "stand-ins." Our claims to know are often like those claims about "triangles" that fail to meet the formal definition of a triangle.

There is another way of construing what's going on when people make ordinary knowledge claims. When I point out to you, after you make the claim that you know that you'll be in Paris this summer, that you might die of a heart attack before then, I suspect your natural reaction will be to shrug your shoulders and retreat to a conditional – "Yeah, of course," you'll say and continue "But provided that doesn't happen (and a whole lot of other stuff like that doesn't happen) then I'll be in Paris this summer." If I'm right, and it is natural to retreat to conditionals in this way, it also seems initially plausible to suppose that it was the conditional we were really claiming to know all along. We don't bother "conditionalizing" everything we claim to know because we don't want to bore our audience to death. Furthermore, one has to be a bit careful with this suggestion. We earlier talked about the truth condition for knowledge. It still seems plausible to suppose that when I claim to know that P, my claim can be correct only if P is true. When I claim to know that I'll be in Paris this summer, I might have (implicitly) in mind only the conditional claim that if nothing unexpected happens then I'll be in Paris, and it might only be the conditional that I need to have conclusive reason to accept. But in addition to the truth of the conditional, I'm suggesting, we should probably understand knowledge claims as implying the truth of the proposition that forms the consequent of the conditional (the part following the "then"). On the view I'm imagining, then, one retains the Cartesian idea that to correctly claim to know that I'll be in Paris, at least the conditional to which I retreat must be supported by reasons so strong that they eliminate any possibility of error. Whether one can find informative conditionals that one can support with that sort of justification is an open question. And the emphasis is on "informative." Certainly, it's not that hard to be justified in believing that P is true if nothing happens to make it false! But it is still informative to tell someone that you know that there is a deer in the backyard (provided that sensation is generally a reliable source of information about the external world, the conditions of perception are normal, I'm not in a place where for some reason people are trying to deceive me with deer replicas, there aren't a lot of deer-like animals around that a person like me couldn't distinguish from a deer, and so on.) The claim is still informative, because it tells you something about the nature of the evidence I do have (my visual experience) for reaching the conclusion I do.

Closure Again

It should already be clear from our discussion of lotteries, but it is worth emphasizing again that if one doesn't require for knowledge justification so strong as to eliminate the possibility of error, then one will have no choice but to abandon at least multi-premise closure, and perhaps even single premise closure. Consider the former. Suppose that we can know Q even though Q has only a probability (relative to our evidence E) of, say, 0.9. We also know R, S, T, U, V, W, X, Y, and Z, where the probability of each relative to our evidence is also 0.9. Probability theory (and common sense) will tell you that even though the probability of each of Q through Z is high, the probability of the conjunction (Q and R and S and T and U and V and W and X and Y and Z) is low (at least if the probability of each proposition is independent of the others). That's why when you are planning a wedding reception you don't assume that all of the invited guests will come even when you have very good reason to believe of each guest that he or she will come. But if we know each of Q through Z and we know that we can deduce the conjunction from the ten premises asserting the conjuncts, then multi-premise closure principles allow us to infer that we are in a position to get knowledge of the conjunction. This is absurd. So it looks as if we must either reject the exceedingly plausible closure principle or go back to strong Cartesian requirements for knowledge.

It's a bit harder to force the dilemma in the case of single premise closure, but it depends on how "weak" one allows standards for knowledge to be. If we allow that we can know Q when its epistemic probability is, say, 0.7 relative to our evidence, and we further allow that we can know that Q entails R even though there is only a 0.7 probability that the entailment holds, then a single-premise closure principle will yield the absurd result that in such a situation one can come to know R

even though R (intuitively) has a probability relative to our evidence of less than 0.5. It might seem initially odd to suppose that the claim that Q entails R can have a probability of less than 1 for someone, but just imagine that the entailment is very complicated and we are relying on an authority who is right only about 70 percent of the time when it comes to really complicated claims of entailment.

So again, if one lets one's standards for knowledge drop low enough, one might need to abandon even single-premise closure for knowledge.[4] The moral one might well draw is that one simply must not let one's standards for knowledge drop too low, even if the price of maintaining high standards is that one rejects as false a great many ordinary knowledge claims.

Gettier Problems

The conclusion that we really can't know a proposition if our epistemic situation leaves open a chance of error is going to be exceedingly unpopular with most philosophers. But there is an additional cost to settling for an account of knowledge that requires for knowledge only epistemically rational or epistemically justified true belief – the famous Gettier problem. Gettier (1963) asked you to consider a person, say, Fred, who has very strong reason to believe the false proposition that Jones own a Ford (P). We can suppose, for example, that unbeknownst to Fred, Jones is a pathological liar who has manufactured all sorts of convincing, but misleading, evidence that he owns a Ford – he shows up at work driving a Ford, shows Fred forged ownership papers, and so on. Having just taken a course in logic, Fred decides to practice his logic and deduces from the proposition that Jones owns a Ford, the proposition that either Jones owns a Ford (P) or Jones is a murderer (Q). Fred has no reason whatsoever to believe that Jones is a murderer, but he has as much reason to believe (P or Q) as he has reason to believe (P). Now suppose through a remarkable coincidence, that while it is false that Jones owns a Ford, it happens to be true that Jones is a murderer, and thus it is true that either Jones owns a Ford or Jones is a murderer. If you think about the situation I've just described, it seems pretty obvious that Fred has a justified true belief that either Jones owns a Ford or Jones is a murderer, but nevertheless doesn't *know* that truth. While Fred had justification for believing a truth, he avoided having a false belief only through a kind of "luck" that seems incompatible with having knowledge.

Note that the counterexample (the hypothetical situation that shows the counterintuitive consequence of the analysis of knowledge) is only possible because we are allowing that the justification sufficient for knowledge need not guarantee the truth of the proposition known. Not to take anything away from Gettier, who put the point in a particularly vivid and effective way, Russell, long before Gettier, also described a situation in which someone has a justified true belief that wasn't knowledge. Russell (1948, p. 154) asked us to imagine a person looking at the proverbial broken clock that reads the correct time twice a day. Our hypothetical person doesn't know that the clock is broken and through a happy coincidence looks at the clock on one of the two occasions when it indicates the correct time. A justified true belief that it is five o'clock results, but again you are supposed to realize that the role luck played precludes the justified true belief's constituting knowledge.

The famous Gettier counterexamples to the "traditional" analysis of knowledge as justified true belief spawned endless articles attempting to add conditions designed to "Gettier-proof" the analysis. The most obvious solution is to insist that in order for someone S to know that P, not only must P be true, but also any crucial premise used in arriving at the conclusion that P must be true. So the revised account of knowledge states that S knows that P when S has a justified true belief arrived at through a chain of reasoning that contains no crucial false premise. That takes care of the example given above, since by hypothesis the person who believed (P or Q) was only justified in believing the disjunction because he was justified in believing the *false* proposition P. It seemed to *some*, however, that we can describe Gettier sorts of situations in which no reasoning (at least *explicit* reasoning) involving falsehoods occurred. In Russell's example, the person looking at the broken clock didn't consciously consider any premise describing the working condition of the clock. Carl Ginet (1975) described the now famous example of someone traveling through a countryside in which, unbeknownst to him, there are a great many "fake" barns – perhaps barn facades built by a Hollywood film company.[6] The person stops his car and happens to look at the *one* genuine barn in the area, forming the justified true belief that there is a barn there. Many epistemologists don't want to allow that this apparently justified true belief constitutes knowledge even though it is hard to identify any false premise that the person employs in reaching his conclusion. Again, the intuition seems to have something to do with the fact that the avoidance of a false belief was a matter of luck.

Whether the above presents a problem for the view that knowledge is just justified true belief arrived at through reasoning that involves "no essential falsehood" is controversial. A great deal depends on how broadly one construes the reasons that support a belief. Certainly, in the barn example, our traveler was not *explicitly* considering the possibility that he was in "fake barn country," nor might he have consciously formed the belief that there is nothing weird about the environment there. But most philosophers also allow that people can believe all sorts of propositions that they don't explicitly consider – such beliefs are sometimes called *dispositional*. You believed five minutes before reading this sentence that 157,734 is greater than 7. But there is a good chance you have never entertained that proposition consciously. That you believed it seems to have something to do with the fact that you would unhesitatingly accept it when you consider it (and perhaps also that you have consciously considered some proposition in the past that implies it).[5] On this conception of belief, it is not all that hard to suppose that we have a great many dispositional beliefs about our environment – most of which never come to the fore of consciousness. In fact, I'm inclined to think that even apparently spontaneous beliefs about our environment are supported by an incredible array of background presuppositions, and if there are critical falsehoods in our background evidence (false propositions which are crucial to our justification) that might be enough to destroy knowledge.

I have talked about just one attempt to deal with the Gettier problem still presupposing that we are on the right track in thinking that knowledge has something to do with justified true belief. Other epistemologists recommend more radical solutions. Goldman, for a while (1967), thought that knowledge had more to do with the cause of someone's belief than the kind of justification the person had in support of that belief. Thinking about Gettier counterexamples, we find that most often the fact that makes true what we believe isn't figuring in the causal chain that produces our belief. In the example of the broken clock, its actually being 5:00 p.m. wasn't part of what causally produced the belief that that was the correct time. The fact that made true (P or Q) in our earlier example was not a fact that played a causal role in our subjects coming to believe that proposition. The causal theory, however, doesn't seem to help much with the fake barn problem. In the example, you will recall, it was a real barn that the person saw and that produced the belief in its existence. Crude causal theories also seem to demand too much for knowledge. If we want to allow, for example, knowledge of the future, we are going to have to modify the causal theory, at least on the assumption that future facts can't cause present beliefs. An obvious modification allows that one can know that P when either the fact that P causes in the right way the belief that

P or some other fact X causes in the right way both the belief that P and the fact that makes P true. Reference to being caused "in the right way" is crucial. It's not hard to imagine situations in which my belief that P is caused by the fact that P but in an odd sort of way that seems quite incompatible with my knowing P. Suppose, for example, that a hypnotist causes me to think that there is a God by making me accept a bad argument for God's existence. Suppose further that there is a God with an odd sense of humor who caused the hypnotist to decide to do this in the first place. Obviously, my belief that God exists was caused, in a roundabout way, by God (the very truth maker for my belief). But it hardly seems right to suppose that I could come to *know* in this way that God exists.

A closely related account of knowledge emphasizes tracking.[7] The crude idea is that S's belief that P constitutes knowledge that P when S's belief tracks the truth of P. This in turn is understood as follows: When S believes that P employing some method of belief acquisition M (say, direct perception), then S's belief that P tracks the truth of P when S wouldn't believe P (through employing that method M) were P false, and would believe (employing that method) P in all situations very similar to the one in which S finds himself. So, for example, on this view, the reason S wouldn't know that it was five o'clock looking at the broken clock is that even if it weren't five o'clock S would still have reached the conclusion that it was. In the case of the person looking at the barn in the countryside surrounded by fake barns, it seems right to suppose that there are similar situations (driving a few hundred yards further down the road) in which one would arrive at the false belief that there is a barn there. A great deal, of course, depends on how we calibrate similarity across possible situations. In any event, tracking theorists like Nozick (1981) have famously denied closure principles for knowledge under known entailment. On the tracking view, one can perhaps know that one is veridically perceiving a tree before one in virtue of the fact that one's belief tracks the fact that one is veridically perceiving the tree. Presumably, one can also know that one's veridically perceiving a tree entails that one is not vividly dreaming of a tree. Yet for all that it might be impossible to know that one is not vividly dreaming of the tree. The idea is that in "close" possible situations in which one isn't veridically perceiving a tree one wouldn't believe that one is. That's on the assumption that the "close possible worlds" in which one doesn't see the tree are worlds in which, for example, one has turned one's head or one has one's eyes closed. To determine whether or not one knows that one is not dreaming, however, one must think about close possible worlds in which one *is* dreaming. In those close worlds, one would presumably continue to believe that one is *not* dreaming (provided that the dream is vivid enough). The belief that one is not dreaming, then, fails to track the fact that one is not.

Proponents of tracking accounts of knowledge hail the rejection of closure as an advantage of their account. They claim that it can accommodate our common sense belief that we know a great many truths while at the same time acknowledging the undeniable force of classic skeptical concerns (discussed in detail in chapter 7). But on the other hand, the appeal of closure principles is itself undeniable. On tracking accounts like Nozick's it turns out that one can imagine situations in which one knows that Jones murdered Smith, but doesn't know that Smith was murdered! Suppose, for example, that Jones did murder Smith and that I found out about it by reading the story in the paper. Jones, however, was part of a huge conspiracy. Had Jones failed in his assassination of Smith, there were a string of back-up assassins ($A2$ through $A20$) each of whom was to carry out the mission in the event of their predecessor failing. If Jones failed, $A2$ would attempt to kill Smith. And if $A2$ failed, then $A3$ would try, and so on until $A20$ gave it his best shot. If any one of the assassins succeeded the rest simply would have fled and the newspaper would have reported correctly the identity of the assassin. However, in the extremely unlikely event that all of the assassins failed, someone trusted by the local papers would call in the false report that Jones had assassinated Smith so as to spread the sort of confusion that might help them make their getaway. If you are still following this complicated story, you should conclude that my belief that Jones murdered Smith did track the relevant fact – in close possible worlds in which Smith wasn't murdered by Jones I would not continue to believe that he was murdered by Jones. But my belief that Smith was murdered does not track the fact that he was because in the closest world in which he wasn't murdered (all of the assassins failed) I would continue to believe that he was. I know through newspaper reports that Jones murdered Smith even though I don't know that Smith was murdered! Can we tolerate any view of knowledge that allows such a possibility?

There is a great deal more that can be said about causal and tracking accounts of knowledge. They are both close cousins of the externalist accounts of justification that we will be considering in subsequent chapters, and we will return to the evaluation of such views in that context (particularly in chapters 5 and 6). For now, however, I want to continue to work on the assumption that knowledge does have something to do with the possession of good epistemic reasons, and I want to return to a claim I made a while ago – the claim that knowledge is not the most fundamental of epistemic concepts.

Epistemic Rationality

If we attempt to understand knowledge as true conviction supported by appropriate epistemic *reasons*, or *evidence* that makes *probable* what we believe, or epistemic *justification*, then we will be committed, rather straightforwardly, to the view that there are epistemic concepts more fundamental than knowledge in terms of which we are trying to understand knowledge. I warned earlier that if we try to explain knowledge employing one of these other concepts, we will need to explain that concept without presupposing an understanding of knowledge. Otherwise, our account will become circular. If knowledge is something like justified true conviction (or conviction supported by good epistemic reasons), then we might also suppose that the most interesting component of knowledge is the justification. After all, the best we can do in living up to our epistemic responsibilities is to conform our belief to what we have good reason to believe. If the world co-operates so as to make those beliefs true, then maybe we'll have knowledge as well. But if it doesn't, we've done the best we can do. It's just our bad (epistemic) luck if it turns out that we are living in the world of *The Matrix*.

It is more than a bit difficult, however, to avoid appealing to our understanding of knowledge in explaining other concepts (like reasons or evidence). Williamson (2000) argues that the best way to understand evidence, for example, appeals to knowledge. Our evidence at a given time simply consists in everything we know. We can talk about what is probable relative to our evidence, but that's just a way of talking about what is probable relative to what we know. If a view like that were correct, then it would be folly to try to explain knowledge by appealing to belief supported by good evidence. In fact, Williamson argues that it is a mistake to suppose that we can analyze knowledge into its component states. He argues, in effect, that knowledge is unanalyzable.[8] In our earlier discussion of analysis, I noted that almost everyone agrees that analysis must end somewhere. There must be some concepts we understand and employ that are the conceptual "building blocks" in terms of which we understand other important ideas or concepts. So it would be foolish to object in principle to a philosopher who takes knowledge to be one of those simple concepts in terms of which we understand others.

Against Williamson, however, it is worth noting that if we understand our epistemic justification, reasons, or evidence in terms of what we know, we'll have a great deal of difficulty even making sense of the common place idea that of the things we at least *claim* to know, some are more probable than others. I might claim to know where I'll be this summer, but I surely have better evidence for thinking that I *exist* right now, than that I'll be in Canada this summer. Given my evidence, it is surely more likely that I exist than that I'll be in Canada this summer. But if all talk of likelihood is relativized to knowledge and I know that I'll be in Canada this summer, then the probability that I'll be in Canada this summer *relative to what I know* (relative to my evidence) should be 1. But again, it's not. Williamson is prepared to "bite the bullet" and claim that all propositions known have an epistemic probability of 1, but it's extraordinarily difficult to reconcile that claim with anything but strong Cartesian requirements for knowledge – requirements that Williamson rejects.

Still, the proof of the proverbial pudding is in the eating. If we don't like the claim that knowledge is the most fundamental of epistemic concepts, the concept in terms of which we are going to understand others, we'll need to develop an alternative view. In the next chapter, we are going to begin our attempt to understand better the concepts of epistemic rationality and justification.

Suggested readings

Butchvarov, Panayot. 1970. *The Concept of Knowledge*, pp. 13–54. Evanston: Northwestern University Press.

Cohen, Stewart. 1999. "Contextualism, Skepticism, and the Structure of Reasons." *Philosophical Perspectives*, 13, 57–89.

Hawthorne, John. 2003. *Knowledge and Lotteries*. Oxford: Clarendon Press.

Notes

1   Again, all this talk of probability will receive a more careful analysis later: there is almost certainly more than one important sense of probability. As we shall also see when we discuss foundationalism, many will insist that we can have knowledge that is not based on evidence in the form of some other proposition known. We will still be able to talk of the probability of a given proposition relative to the justification the person possesses.

2   There are philosophers who doubt that descriptions of the future even have a truth value (are either true or false).

3   This is the basis of the well-known preface paradox. The author declares in the preface that there are bound to be errors in the book. Presumably, the author takes each claim made in the book to be true, but is wise enough to realize that it is highly unlikely that they are all true.

4   I'm indebted to Tim McGrew for helpful comments that informed this discussion.

5   The precise analysis is going to be complicated. This is a topic to which we will return later. I suspect that the correct analysis of dispositional belief must lean heavily on the idea that dispositions have grounds. The ground of the solubility of sugar is its chemical composition. The ground of a dispositional belief, one might argue, is some relatively stable property of the believer that is the effect of some past conscious consideration and acceptance of a proposition.

6   Ginet first introduced the example in discussion with Alvin Goldman at a University of Michigan faculty colloquium in the mid-1960s. It also appears in Ginet (1988).

7   Its most well-known proponent is Nozick (1981).

8   He argues that the failure of philosophers to analyze knowledge in such a way as to avoid Gettier problems is one strong indication that there is no correct analysis. Of course, if one doesn't provide an analysis of knowledge, it is only in an odd sense that one avoids the Gettier problem. I never lost a chess game to a grandmaster, but that's only because I don't play grandmasters.

Chapter 3

Epistemic Rationality and its Structure

I argued in the last chapter that the concept of epistemic rationality or justification may be more fundamental to epistemology than the concept of knowledge. This would obviously be true if the justification S has for believing P is partially *constitutive* of S's knowing that P. But even if one cannot define knowledge in terms of justification, the concept of a belief's being rational or justified is independently interesting and fundamental to the study of epistemology.

Justification and Normativity

In chapter 1 we emphasized that the epistemologist is primarily interested in *epistemic* reasons or justification for belief. There may be prudential or moral reasons for holding a belief, but they are not the primary focus of the epistemologist. It is important to keep this point in mind in assessing the common claim that justification and rationality are *normative* concepts. In chapter 1, I contrasted metaepistemology and applied epistemology, and I noted that applied epistemological questions are often also called "normative." I avoid that term because it is not at all clear to me what philosophers have in mind by characterizing a concept as normative. Sometimes philosophers seem to start with a list of expressions whose meaning is paradigmatically normative and then view as normative any expression whose meaning can be even partially explicated using one of the terms on the list. The list might be long or short depending on whether we think that all normative expressions can be defined in terms of a relatively few fundamental "core" normative notions. So one might include among the paradigmatically normative expressions such terms as "good," "ought," "should," "right," "permissible," "obligatory," and their opposites.

If we proceed in this fashion, it does look as if epistemic justification and rationality are normative concepts. It is certainly the case that epistemologists often seem quite comfortable interchanging questions about whether or not evidence *E* justifies one in believing *P* with questions about whether or not one *should* believe *P* on the basis of *E*. We might say it would be *wrong* to believe *P* if there is no reason to believe it. Our justified beliefs are those that are *permissible* for us to have. As Plantinga (1992) points out in discouraging epistemologists from obsessing about justification, the very etymology of the word "justification" certainly suggests that we are dealing with a *value* term. But it should be clear after our distinction between epistemic reasons/justification and other sorts of reasons/justification that this way of explaining what is meant by characterizing epistemic concepts as normative is not exactly helpful. It may be that we *morally* ought to believe *P*, or *prudentially* ought to believe *P* even if we epistemically ought not to believe *P*. It is the moral "ought" and its close cousin the prudential "ought" that are probably the real paradigms of normative expressions, and it is not at all clear that the epistemic "ought" has a meaning analogous to these other "oughts."

Richard Foley (1987) argues that we can define epistemic justification/rationality in terms of what one ought to believe and that one can view different "oughts" as species of a common genus. Crudely, his idea is that all normative judgments, judgments about what one ought to do or believe, are judgments assessing the efficacy of achieving goals or ends. There are different kinds of normative judgments concerning what we ought to do and what we ought to believe because there are different goals or ends that we are concerned to emphasize in making those judgments. Thus when we are talking about *morally* justified action, the relevant goal might be something like creating good and avoiding evil. When we are concerned with what *prudence* dictates, the relevant goals might include anything that is desired for its own sake. What one legally ought to do is a function of the extent to which an action satisfies the goal of following the law. Foley's suggestion was that judgments about what one *epistemically* ought to believe are concerned with how well the belief achieves the dual goals of believing what is true and avoiding belief in what is false.

I can't do justice to the complexities of Foley's view here, but I do want to suggest that the view faces serious objections. Consider again the paradigm of a non-epistemic reason. Consider, for example, a patient who is told that if she can get herself to believe that she will recover from the devastating cancer ravaging her body, that will at least increase the probability that she will recover. That might give the patient a strong reason to try to acquire the belief even if it is not epistemically rational to believe that she will get well – the odds for even the optimist are long. But let us suppose that by forming the relevant belief, the patient produces for herself a long life devoted to scientific and philosophical investigation, investigation that results in an enormous number of true beliefs. Despite accomplishing the goal of believing what is true through believing that she will get well, our patient (by hypothesis) had no *epistemic* reason to believe that she would get well.

The obvious solution (one suggested by Foley) is to restrict the relevant epistemic goal to that of *now* believing what is true and *now* avoiding belief in what is false. But such a revision doesn't really solve the problem. Suppose there is an all-powerful being who will immediately cause me to believe massive falsehoods now unless I accept the proposition that there are mermaids. It would seem that again I could accomplish the goal of now avoiding belief in what is false by believing that there are mermaids. Again, by hypothesis, that doesn't make the belief any more *epistemically* rational.

Of course, one really wants to define the epistemic "ought" not in terms of what actually *does* or *would* accomplish the goal of believing what is true, but rather in terms of what one is *justified* in believing will accomplish the goal of now believing what is true with respect to a given proposition. But if we do this, we immediately see that we aren't really getting anywhere trying to *explain* justification in terms of what one ought to believe when we are interested in getting at the truth. If anything, it is the other way around. We can explain the epistemic "ought" only if we have some prior grasp of what it is for a belief to be epistemically justified.

There are other ways of trying to understand the alleged normative character of epistemic justification/reasons, but I'm not convinced any are illuminating. One might suppose that when one characterizes a belief as justified one is indicating that it is not appropriate to *criticize* the belief. By contrast, when one says of a belief that it is unjustified or irrational, one *is* criticizing the belief. But for the view to gain even initial plausibility, it would be important to distinguish the criticism of a belief from the criticism of the subject who holds the belief. It is simply false that we would always criticize a person for holding a belief we judge to be epistemically irrational. We might, for example, conclude that the person is just too stupid to be able to evaluate properly the relevant evidence and we might, as a result, seldom criticize him for the many wildly irrational beliefs he holds. To be sure, epistemically irrational beliefs are in *some* way *defective* – they are epistemically defective! But it hardly seems that this sheds much light on what it is for a belief to be epistemically irrational.

I have spent a fair bit of time on questions concerning the alleged normativity of epistemic judgments, because it is important to think clearly about some of these matters when we later assess some of the internalism/externalism controversies concerning the nature of epistemic justification.

Having Justification for a Belief and Having a Justified Belief

We briefly noted in chapter 1 a distinction between there being good epistemic reason for S to believe some proposition P and S's having a justified belief that P. It seems obvious that in some sense you might have good reason to believe that your plane won't crash, even though you are one of those unfortunate fliers who can't quite get yourself to believe what you might even know you have good reason to believe. You have justification for believing that your plane won't crash, then, but you don't believe, let alone have a justified belief, that your plane won't crash. Which concept should be of most interest to the epistemologist – having justification or having a justified belief?

It is at least tempting to suppose that there being justification for S to believe P is conceptually more fundamental than S's having a justified belief that P. This is so because it is tempting to suppose that one can understand having a justified belief only if one understands the concept of there being justification for S to believe P. Specifically, it is tempting to suppose that S's belief that P is justified just in case S's belief that P is based on the good epistemic reasons (the justification) S has to believe P. It is also plausible (though controversial) to suppose that for a belief to be based on reasons one possesses, that belief must be caused by, or causally sustained by, those reasons.

There is another reason that epistemologists interested in applied epistemology are probably well advised to focus on what there is justification for people to believe rather than which beliefs are actually justified. If it is true that S's belief is justified only if it is based on good reasons, and it is also true that basing is to be understood, even partially, in terms of causation, then it is not clear that philosophers, in their capacity as philosophers, are particularly well equipped to answer questions concerning which beliefs are justified. The causes of belief are a more appropriate subject for the psychologist. Freud spent a great deal of time wondering what causes belief in a God or in an afterlife. The epistemologist, qua epistemologist, should find such speculation utterly uninteresting. Whatever causes such beliefs, the epistemologist's concern is with the question of whether we possess good reasons for believing the propositions in question. To answer that question we need not concern ourselves with what is actually causing our beliefs. We will need to remind ourselves of this fact when we later attempt to locate the precise content of the internalist's claims about the nature of justification.

The Structure of Justification

Quite understandably, you might be getting a bit impatient waiting for a positive account of epistemic rationality or justification. But at the risk of trying your patience a bit more, I want to postpone a more detailed answer to that question by focusing first on structural questions concerning the nature of epistemic justification and rationality. If knowledge is partly to be understood in terms of justification, then some of these structural questions will also apply to knowledge. But even if knowledge cannot be defined in terms of justified belief, structural controversies concerning the nature of justification may be paralleled by similar controversies concerning the nature of knowledge.

But how is all this talk about the structure of justification or knowledge to be understood? *Foundationalism*, perhaps the most famous theory of epistemic justification, explicitly employs a structural metaphor. All justification (and all knowledge), the foundationalist claims, rests on a foundation of noninferential (direct, basic) justification (knowledge). One gets radically different versions of foundationalism depending on how the foundationalist understands the critical concept of noninferential justification. While *traditional* versions of foundationalism have fallen on hard times, externalist analogues that retain a foundationalist structure are presently very popular. In that sense, structural foundationalism is still probably the received view in epistemology.

Foundationalism

If we think about most of our beliefs that we take to be rational, it seems plausible to suggest that their rationality is owed to the fact that we justifiably believe other different propositions. So, for example, I take myself to have good reason to believe that Brutus killed Caesar, but only because I justifiably believe (among other things) that various generally reliable historical texts describe the event. I have good reason to believe that it rained last night, but only because when I went outside this morning I noticed that the ground was sopping wet. We are discussing the structure of epistemic justification here, but one could make the same point about knowledge. It seems that most of the truths we know we know only because we are in a position to infer those truths from other propositions we know. When our justification for believing P consists, in part, in the having of other justified beliefs, let us say that the justification is inferential. [When our knowledge that P is constituted in part by our knowing other propositions, we can call that knowledge inferential.] When we call the justification and knowledge inferential, [we are implying that the justification and knowledge involve inference from other propositions justifiably believed or known.]

Foundationalists want to contrast inferential justification/knowledge with a kind of justification/knowledge that is not constituted, in whole or in part, by the having of other justified beliefs/other knowledge. Let us call this other sort of justification/knowledge, noninferential justification/knowledge. But why should we suppose that there is a kind of justification that is different from inferential justification? Why should we suppose that we can rationally believe a proposition if we can cite no evidence for our belief in the form of other propositions from which we can legitimately infer the proposition in question?

The principle of inferential justification

Suppose I tell you to make no plans for the weekend, as the earth will be destroyed tomorrow. I offer as my evidence for this startling conclusion the claim that there is a giant asteroid that will smash into earth in about five hours. Naturally alarmed, you ask me what reason I have for thinking that there is this asteroid on a collision course with Earth. I respond that it is just a hunch on my part. As soon as you discover that I have no epistemic justification at all for believing that the asteroid exists, you will immediately conclude that my bizarre conclusion about the fate of Earth is wildly irrational. (An exactly parallel discussion might have taken place involving knowledge claims). Generalizing from examples like this, one might suggest the following principle:

> To be justified in believing P on the basis of E one must be justified in believing.

The basic idea behind the principle is just that one can't get something from nothing. When we attempt to expand our justified beliefs or knowledge through inference, we will succeed only if the premises from which we infer our conclusions are themselves justified or known. Garbage in – garbage out. The principle is so plausible that philosophers with widely differing accounts of justification and knowledge accept it.

Now consider another example. Suppose I claim to be justified in believing that Fred will die shortly and I offer as my justification that a certain line across his palm (the infamous "lifeline") is short. Rightly skeptical, you wonder what reason I have for believing that palm lines have anything whatsoever to do with length of life. As soon as you become satisfied that I have no justification for supposing that there is any kind of probabilistic connection between the character of this line and Fred's life, you will again reject my claim to have a reasonable belief about Fred's impending demise. That suggests that we might expand our principle concerning inferential justification to include a second clause:

> To be justified in believing P on the basis of E one must be justified in believing that E makes probable P (where E's entailing P can be viewed as the upper limit of making probable).

We can combine the two principles into what I have frequently called the principle of inferential justification (PIJ):

To have justification for believing P on the basis of E one must have not only (1) justification for believing E, but also (2) justification for believing that E makes probable P.

Clause (2) of the principle is far more controversial than clause (1). In fact, it is probably rejected by most epistemologists. As we'll see later, clause (2) demands a great deal for inferential justification and is, consequently, a potent weapon in the arsenal of the skeptic, who will wield it mercilessly in an attempt to convince you that you lack much of the inferential justification you might have thought you possessed. A principle with the potential to cause this much trouble should be accepted only after very careful consideration. But despite the fact that it might prove a liability in attempting to respond to the skeptic, what reason could one have for rejecting clause (2) of the principle of inferential justification? Doesn't the example given above (and countless others like it) suggest that we do, in fact, accept the principle? Isn't it precisely because we don't think astrologers, entrails readers, palm readers, and the like, have reason to believe that their premises make probable their conclusions that we reject their conclusions as irrational? The answer to this question is far more complicated than it might initially seem and we shall address it in much more detail in chapter 6 when we evaluate the view that I call inferential internalism.

Regress arguments for foundationalism

Let us return to the question of why we should suppose that there is a kind of justification other than inferential justification. The most famous argument for foundationalism is the regress argument. In fact, however, I think that there are two quite different regress arguments for foundationalism – an epistemic regress argument and a conceptual regress argument. The former is the most common, perhaps, so let us begin with it.

The epistemic regress argument

If all justification were inferential, then for someone S to have justification for believing some proposition P, S must be in a position to legitimately infer it from some other proposition $E1$. But if the first, relatively uncontroversial, clause of the principle of inferential justification is true, then $E1$ could give S epistemic reason to believe P only if S were justified in believing $E1$. But if all justification were inferential, the only way for S to be justified in believing $E1$ would to be to infer it from some other proposition $E2$ that S has good reason to believe. If all justification were inferential, however, the only way S could be justified in believing $E2$ would be for S to justifiably infer it from some other proposition $E3$ which is justifiably believed, and so on, *ad infinitum*. But finite beings cannot complete an infinitely long chain of reasoning and so, if all justification were inferential, no-one would be justified in believing anything at all to any extent whatsoever. This most radical of all skepticisms is absurd (it entails that one couldn't even be justified in believing it) and so there must be a kind of justification that is not inferential, i.e. there must be noninferentially justified beliefs which terminate regresses of justification.

If the more controversial second clause of PIJ is correct, the looming regresses proliferate. Not only must S above be justified in believing $E1$, S must also be justified in believing that $E1$ makes probable P, a proposition that would have to be inferred (if there are no foundations) from some other proposition $F1$, which would have to be inferred from $F2$, and so on, *ad infinitum*. But S would also need to be justified in believing that $F1$ does in fact make likely that $E1$ makes likely P, a proposition he would need to infer from some other proposition $G1$, which he would need to infer from some other proposition *G2* ... And *S* would need to infer that *G1* does indeed make likely that *F1* makes likely that *E1* makes likely *P* ... Without noninferential justification, it would seem that we would need to complete an infinite number of infinitely long chains of reasoning in order to be justified in believing anything.

The conceptual regress argument

The epistemic regress argument discussed above relies on the unacceptability of a vicious *epistemic* regress. But one might also argue, more fundamentally, that without a *concept* of noninferential justification, one faces a vicious conceptual regress. What precisely is our understanding of inferential justification? What makes the principle of inferential justification true (with or without its controversial second clause)? It is at least tempting to answer that question by suggesting that the principle of inferential justification is analytic (true by definition). It is just part of what it means, one might argue, to say of someone that he has inferential justification for believing some proposition *P*, that he can legitimately infer *P* from some other proposition *E1* that is justifiably believed. But if this is a plausible suggestion, if this is a plausible account of the very idea of inferential justification, we face another potentially vicious regress, this time a conceptual regress. Our understanding of inferential justification seems to presuppose an understanding of justification.

Consider an analogy. The vast majority of things we take to be good (exercise, regular physical checkups, a good salary) we think of as good only as means. Things are good as means, we might say, when they lead to something that is good. Now suppose a philosopher defines being good as a means this way and then goes on to claim that the *only* way something can be good is to be good as a means. There seems to be something seriously wrong with such a view. Of course, we might worry about how we could ever know that anything is good as a means, given that it might seem to require an infinitely long search for more and more good things. But there is a more fundamental concern, and that is that if we tried to understand all goodness as merely instrumental goodness, we would never locate the conceptual *source* of goodness. Our analysis of being good as a means presupposes an understanding of being good. To avoid being charged with a vicious regress, we would need to introduce the notion of something's being good in itself. Indeed, it is commonplace in ethics to argue that unless we had an understanding of something's being intrinsically good, we couldn't even form the idea of something's being

41

good as a means (instrumentally good). Similarly, the foundationalist may argue that without an understanding of noninferential justification, we are not even in a position to form the concept of inferential justification.

In the much more technical language of philosophers, the solution to the problem of conceptual regress is to understand inferential justification (and knowledge) *recursively.* What's a recursive definition? Well, consider the idea of being a descendent of X. How shall we define being a descendant? Is it being the child of X? No. That's one way to be a descendent of X, but we can be a descendent of X and be further removed than that. Is it to be the child of X or the child of a child of X? Not that either, of course. It is to be the child of X, or the child of a child of X, or the child of a child of a child of X, or, . . . , and so on *ad infinitum.* We understand the infinitely long pattern and thus understand what it is to be a descendent of X. Being the child of X is the *base clause* in our recursive definition. It is the recurring concept understanding of which is presupposed in each of the disjuncts in our infinitely complex disjunction (complex "or" statement). In exactly the same way, the foundationalist does (or should) want to understand noninferential justification as the base clause for a recursive definition of justification. To be justified in believing P is to be noninferentially justified in believing P, or for P to be justifiably inferred from some proposition E that we are noninferentially justified in believing, or to be . . . and so on *ad infinitum.*

The conceptual regress argument is not uncontroversial. One might claim that there is a generic concept of justification – one not defined in terms of noninferential justification, which in turn can be used to set out conditions for inferential justification. In like fashion, I suppose one could claim that there is no such thing as intrinsic goodness. Instrumental goodness is, to be sure, defined in such a way that it presupposes an understanding of being good, but the concept of being good is not itself to be defined by appeal to the idea of intrinsic goodness. Perhaps it is indefinable. Perhaps it has some other definition.

One can't rule out the formal possibility raised by the above response to the conceptual regress argument. But it is just that – a formal possibility. The foundationalist has an exceedingly plausible suggestion for how to define inferential justification based on models of definition we understand very well. It is, at the very least, incumbent upon those who reject the account but who accept some version of the principle of inferential justification (with or without its controversial second clause) to come up with that generic definition of justification for use in trying to say something useful about the conditions required for inferential justification.

42

Responses to the Epistemic Regress Argument and Alternatives to Foundationalism

There seem to be only three real alternatives to embracing the epistemic regress argument for foundationalism. The first is the so-called *coherence* theory of justification. The second is a view that Peter Klein (1999) calls *infinitism*. The third is radical *skepticism*.

The Coherence Theory of Justification

The coherence theorists live by the slogan that the only thing that can justify a belief is another belief. They reject the foundationalist's idea that there can be epistemically rational beliefs whose justification is not owed to the having of other beliefs. The foundationalist's mistake, the coherence theorist argues, is to suppose that justification is *linear*. Our justification for believing *P* does involve the having of other beliefs, but it is not constituted by the having of other beliefs that are justified *prior* to believing *P*, beliefs from which we can generate the justification for believing *P*. As the name for the view implies, the coherence theorist argues that the epistemic justification for a belief that *P* consists in the way that *P* coheres with other propositions believed.

Perhaps the best model for the coherence theory is the puzzle. Imagine a puzzle made for masochists. The pieces are all precisely the same shape, each piece capable of fitting with every other piece. The instructions for the puzzle include only that there is a way of fitting the pieces together that will result in a beautiful picture. If after decades of working at the puzzle you finally put together a picture of a beautiful schooner with white clouds overhead and a rock shore line in the distance, you might be more than a bit put off by a friend who wonders why you think you've got the pieces in the right place. The answer to your friend's question is that the position of each piece in the puzzle is justified by virtue of the fact that when it is put where it is relative to the placement of the other pieces, the nice, coherent picture is formed. In like fashion, the coherence theorist argues, [each belief in our attempt to represent (picture) reality is justified by virtue of the fact that the belief, together with the other beliefs we have, form a nice, coherent picture of the way things are.] My belief that Washington was the first president of the United States, for example, is justified because it fits well with all sorts of other beliefs I have – my belief that history books are generally reliable and that they contain references to Washington as the first president, my belief that there is a monument in Washington, DC, celebrating Washington's presidency, and so on.

We can distinguish pure and impure coherence theories of justification. A pure coherence theory takes the justification of every belief to be a matter of its coherence with other propositions believed. An impure theory restricts the thesis to a subclass of beliefs. BonJour (1985), for example, defended a coherence theory of epistemic justification for empirical beliefs only.[1] There is nothing in principle to prevent a coherence theorist from restricting the theory to an even more narrow subclass of beliefs.

The vast majority of philosophers who support a coherence theory of justification take the relevant beliefs with which a given justified belief must cohere to be those present in a single individual. What justifies S in believing P is that P coheres with some set of propositions that S either occurrently or dispositionally believes.[2] What justifies *you* in believing P is P's coherence with other propositions that you believe. But while epistemic justification relativized to an *individual's* belief system is the norm for coherence theories, one finds at least some interest in what we might call a social coherence theory. Roughly, the idea is that what justifies S in believing P is a matter not just of what S believes, but of what others in the community believe. A very crude social coherence theory of epistemic justification might hold that S is justified in believing P only if P coheres with the propositions believed by all or most members of S's community. Because one can distinguish as many different communities as one likes, epistemic justification on this view must always be relativized to a given community. In addition to actual individuals and communities, one can develop a kind of hypothetical individual or community coherence theory of justification. One can try to define the justification S has for believing P in terms of the way P coheres with the propositions that S would believe or S's community would believe were S or his community to engage in some sort of prolonged intellectual investigation. For simplicity, we will focus on the kind of coherence theories that relativize epistemic justification to an individual's belief system, but most of what we say will apply with appropriate modifications to other versions of the view.

Once we are clear about which beliefs a given belief must cohere with in order to be epistemically justified, we'll need more information from the coherence theorist about what constitutes coherence. Often, the coherence theorist will begin by claiming that coherence must minimally involve logical consistency (lack of explicit contradiction), but go on to concede that consistency is far too weak a relation to constitute the glue

44

of coherence. After all, one can imagine a person with a thousand beliefs none of which has anything to do with any of the others, but where each proposition believed is consistent with the conjunction of the others. So, for example, suppose that I believe that Paris is in France, snow is white, and there are zebra in Africa. These three beliefs are perfectly consistent with one another, but they don't seem to support each other. If I add to these three beliefs indefinitely many others all of which are similarly unrelated, the resulting belief system hardly seems a paradigm of a coherent belief system. Mere consistency among one's beliefs doesn't seem to be sufficient for a coherence that would render beliefs justified.

Furthermore, perhaps surprisingly, it is not at all obvious that consistency among our beliefs is even *necessary* for those beliefs being justified. Appealing again to lottery-type situations, Foley (1979) argues that we can easily think of a set of inconsistent beliefs each of which is perfectly justified. If there are a thousand people in a lottery that I know to be fair, I can justifiably believe of each participant that he or she will lose and also justifiably believe that not all of them will lose. None of these beliefs is consistent with the conjunction of the rest, but each seems perfectly justified. The problem isn't restricted to literal lotteries. As we noted in discussing closure principles, when planning for a wedding, you might be perfectly justified in believing of each of the good friends you invite that he or she will attend, but you would be a fool to believe that they will all attend. It is reasonable to believe that the best free throw shooter in the NBA will make his next free throw, and that he will make the free throw after that, and the one after that, and so on, but it is wildly irrational to believe that he will make all of his free throws over the course of a season. So the coherence theorist is wrong to tell us that a belief of ours is epistemically rational only if it is consistent with the rest of what we believe.

A closely related problem concerns the possibility of admitting into one's belief system a necessary falsehood *F*. If one believes even one necessary falsehood (e.g. that $7 + 5 = 11$), then none of one's beliefs will be consistent with the rest of what one believes – the conjunction of a necessary falsehood with any other proposition is itself a necessary falsehood. It seems more than a little harsh, however, to let your making one philosophical or mathematical error destroy the possibility of *any* epistemic justification for believing *any* proposition.

Coherence theorists are typically wary of requiring too much for the coherence of a belief system. So, for example, one might initially suppose that an ideal model of a coherent belief system might be one in which [each proposition believed is entailed by the conjunction of the rest] But such proposals are usually dismissed with the observation that such a requirement would be too difficult to satisfy (BonJour, 1985). In fact, however, the problem is precisely the opposite. It is far too easy to satisfy the requirement. In fact, if we include dispositional beliefs, I can confidently claim to have a belief system in which each of my beliefs is entailed by the rest of what I believe. And the same is, or should be true of everyone who has taken and remembers a course in elementary logic. If I believe P and I believe Q (for any P and Q), I should also believe (P or not-Q) and (Q or not-P).[3] But P and (Q or not-P) entails Q, and Q and (P or not-Q) entails P. In an utterly trivial way it will turn out that each proposition I believe is entailed by the conjunction of every other proposition I believe. Again, that hardly seems to guarantee that I've got an epistemically ideal system of beliefs.

The coherence theorist will no doubt be tempted to reply to the above observation by arguing that the belief in the disjunction (P or not-Q) is entirely parasitic upon the *prior* belief in P, but once one abandons a linear conception of justification, it is not clear what sort of epistemic priority P is supposed to have over (P or not-Q) just because the belief that P may have preceded in time the belief that (P or not-Q).

Ironically, perhaps probabilistic connections provide a stronger "glue" for coherence than logical relations. So a coherence theorist might claim that a system of beliefs increases its coherence the more the propositions believed stand in probabilistic connections with each other. Explanatory coherence theorists emphasize the importance of having a belief system in which one maximizes the number of propositions believed where one has within one's belief system propositions that can explain the propositions believed. So on this view, ancient people might have had justification for believing that there was once a great flood in part because that hypothesis would explain well, and thus cohere well, with another hypothesis they accepted – that there were fossilized remains of fish skeletons in areas that were nowhere near water. It's difficult, however, to regard entailment as anything other than the upper limit of making probable and if it is too easy to come by a belief system in which each proposition believed is entailed by the rest, it is hard to see how one can avoid the problem by emphasizing probability.

There are enough powerful arguments against coherence theories of justification that one need not turn to problematic concerns. And some objections to a coherence theory do seem to miss the mark. So, for example, some seem to be concerned with the fact that the coherence theorist embraces a radical relativization of justification. Your belief that P might cohere wonderfully with the rest of what you believe, while my belief that not-*P* might cohere wonderfully with the rest of what I believe. If so, then you will be justified in believing *P* (relative to your system of beliefs) while I am justified in believing not-*P* (relative to my system of beliefs). But this is hardly a problem for the coherence theorist. Any plausible account of epistemic justification will acknowledge that one person *S* can be justified in believing *P* while another *R* is justified in believing not-*P*. The traditional foundationalist who traces all justification back to noninferentially justified beliefs (typically to noninferentially justified beliefs about the character of experiences) will allow that you can be justified in believing *P* while I'm justified in believing not-*P*. Your foundational justification might simply be different from mine – you might have had different experiences than I have had. After having had an apparent conversation with one, you might have good reason to believe that there are leprechauns. In the absence of such experience, I might have no epistemic reason at all to believe in the existence of such creatures.

There is also the vague concern that a coherence theory of justification makes one's choice of what to believe too "subjective" or too "arbitrary." I want to know what to believe and the coherence theorist tells me to come up with a coherent set of beliefs. But for every coherent set of propositions I entertain, I can think of another set inconsistent with the first but just as internally coherent. Won't this make the epistemic choice of what to believe implausibly arbitrary? But coherence theorists will reply that we are, no doubt, *caused* to believe firmly certain propositions, and given that we find ourselves with certain beliefs that we can't get rid of, and given that we are trying to determine whether or not to hold still others, it is not clear that the coherence theorist leaves us with no guidance. To be sure, if we had no beliefs *at all*, and we were trying to get "started" with beliefs, the coherence theory might be perfectly silent with respect to how to choose a non-arbitrary starting position. But that is simply not the world in which any real-life believers find themselves.[4]

A similar response can be made to those who worry that the coherence theorist somehow cuts us off from the world that makes true or false our beliefs. Nothing in the theory, however, precludes the possibility of our beliefs being caused by features of a belief-independent world. The epistemological coherence theory holds only that whatever the cause of our beliefs, their epistemic status is a function solely of coherence.

There is one other potentially devastating problem facing the coherence theory of justification. Ironically, the problem was highlighted most effectively by BonJour (1985) in the course of defending the view (before he converted to foundationalism). The problem is related to the internalism/externalism controversy that we will be discussing later. For now, however, we need only point out that there are two importantly different versions of the coherence theory of justification. On one version, a belief is epistemically justified provided that it coheres with the rest of what is believed. On the other, a belief is epistemically justified provided that the believer is aware that (knows that, has a justified belief that) the belief coheres with the rest of what is believed. The first version isn't very plausible. If a person believes a set of propositions that cohere wonderfully when the person has no way of discovering the connections between what he believes, in what sense are the person's beliefs justified? Suppose, for example, that I decide to believe every proposition I hear asserted by a person with red hair. Through some miraculous coincidence, the propositions I end up believing employing this method cohere wonderfully. Each is made probable by some conjunction of the others. Being stupid enough to believe assertions simply because they were made by red-haired people, I also have no clue as to what the evidential connections are between the propositions I believe. Would anyone suppose that my good fortune in arriving at a coherent system of beliefs translates into my having justified beliefs?

So coherence without awareness of coherence seems hopeless as a source of epistemic justification. But if we insist that a belief is justified only when the believer is aware of that belief's cohering with the rest of what is believed (call that view *access* coherentism), we need some account of how to understand awareness of a belief's cohering with other beliefs. Minimally, that will require some account of how it is that we figure out what we believe, and how it is that we discover connections between propositions believed. Pure coherence theorists have only one source of justification – coherence. The only way to figure out what you believe would be to notice a coherence between the proposition that you have a certain belief and other propositions believed. But to realize that that coherence obtains, you would again need to notice a coherence between the proposition that you believe that you have a certain belief and the rest of what you believe, and so on, *ad infinitum*. An exactly analogous problem concerns awareness of the connections between propositions believed. To justify our belief that a given evidential connection obtains, we would need to discover coherence between our belief that the evidential connection obtains and the rest of what we believe. But discovering that coherence would require that we discover another coherence between our belief about coherence and the rest of what we believe, and so on *ad infinitum*. Ironically, a coherence theory designed specifically to avoid the regress argument for foundationalism faces its own vicious regress.

Infinitism

The epistemic regress argument relies on the premise that finite beings cannot complete an infinitely long chain of reasoning. Klein (1998, 1999) defends a view he calls infinitism. The infinitist refuses the foundationalist's invitation to embrace the concept of noninferential justification but wonders whether finite beings don't have more resources than one might first suppose. While we may not be able to actually complete a chain of reasoning that is infinitely long, we may very well have the *capacity* to come up with each of infinitely many arguments for each of infinitely many premises, and such a capacity is all that is required for us to be inferentially justified in believing infinitely many propositions. Earlier, we distinguished occurrent from dispositional belief. There is nothing absurd in the supposition that people have an infinite number of justified beliefs (most of which are not, of course, conscious at any given time). You believe and believe justifiably that 2 is greater than 1, that 3 is greater than 1, that 4 is greater than 1, and so on *ad infinitum*. With an infinite number of beliefs at their disposal, there is nothing absurd about suggesting that people are in a position to offer a legitimate argument for every proposition they believe.

The idea behind infinitism is intriguing, but we should begin a careful evaluation of the view by noting that having inferential justification for believing *P* involves more than being able to infer *P* from other propositions believed. Minimally, we argued earlier, one would need to infer *P* from other propositions *justifiably* believed. The infinitist now faces the conceptual regress argument discussed earlier. The very concept of inferential justification seems to require some prior understanding of epistemic justification. Klein thinks that one can avoid the conceptual regress argument by rejecting the basic idea behind a recursive analysis of justification. At the very least, however, he owes us an account – a plausible account – of the generic understanding of justification to which he must appeal.

There is another problem, however, that faces both infinitism and the coherence theory of justification. While the foundationalist has faced a wide array of criticisms aimed at specific accounts of noninferential justification (some of which we will consider in the next chapter), there is surely something compelling about the idea that there are some propositions that we have perfectly good reason to believe – indeed that we know – even though we would think it a kind of joke to suppose that we need to supply some evidence for those beliefs in the form of other different propositions believed. You kick me really hard in the shin and I immediately realize that I feel intense pain. I know that I'm in pain. It's about as reasonable a belief as one can have. But do I need to infer that I'm in pain from something else I reasonably believe?! It is not that I couldn't muster up an argument if I had to. Blood is dripping down my leg and I seem to be screaming at the top of my lungs. Most often when all that's going on I'm in intense pain. Right. But it is literally a joke to suppose that my reason for thinking that I'm in pain requires noticing anything about blood or screaming. The coherence theorist thinks that my belief that I'm in pain is justified if it coheres well with the rest of what I believe – the access coherence theorist thinks that the belief is justified if I am aware of the fact that the belief coheres well with the rest of what I believe. But it just isn't remotely plausible to suppose that my access to my pain has anything whatsoever to do with coherence among my beliefs. It's not that the coherence might not exist – it's just that it surely has nothing to do with the reason I have for thinking that I'm in pain – a reason that is much more immediate than anything suggested by relations of coherence among beliefs.

Radical Skepticism

The third alternative to foundationalism as a response to the threat of regress is a radical skepticism – indeed, the most radical of all skepticisms. The foundationalist argues that unless there is noninferential justification we have no justification for believing anything at all. Of course, a philosopher can accept that claim and go on to argue that since there is no such thing as noninferential justification, we have no justification for believing anything at all! Understandably, perhaps, this most radical form of skepticism has not been taken seriously by many in the history of philosophy. Perhaps its most obvious problem is that any argument for the view appears to be epistemically self-refuting. An argument is epistemically self-refuting if the truth of its conclusion entails that one couldn't possibly have any reason to believe its premises. Any argument that concludes that we have no reason for believing anything is obviously epistemically self-refuting in this sense. We'll talk more about epistemic self-refutation later. It is not clear that one can simply ignore an argument after noticing that it has a self-defeating nature. After all, if you believe the premises of the argument and the premises of the argument entail the conclusion that you have no reason to believe those premises, then you've got a problem and you'd better figure out what to do about it. We will try to do more justice to skeptical arguments later in this book. But for now, we might observe only that most philosophers will take radical skepticism to be a view that one should accept only if one is driven towards it. If we can't find a plausible way of understanding noninferential justification, and we can't embrace an alternative solution to the regress problems, then, but only then, should we let regress drive us to radical skepticism.

Beyond Structure

The reader might well find all this discussion about the structure of justification just a tad abstract. Foundationalists think that there is such a thing as noninferential justification and that all justified beliefs owe their justification ultimately to noninferentially justified beliefs. But obviously we need a metaepistemological account of what would render a belief noninferentially justified, and an applied account of which beliefs are noninferentially justified. Even if we find foundations for justification and knowledge, we will also need to figure out how we can legitimately move beyond our foundations to the rest of what we justifiably believe. To these questions we now turn.

Suggested readings

BonJour, Laurence. 1985. *The Structure of Empirical Justification*, chapters 2 and 5. Cambridge, MA: Harvard University Press.

DePaul, Michael, ed., 2001. *Resurrecting Old-Fashioned Foundationalism*. Lanham, MD: Rowman and Littlefield.

Klein, Peter. 1998. "Foundationalism and the Infinite Regress of Reasons." *Philosophy and Phenomenological Research*, 58 (4), 919–25.

Notes

1   The paradigm of an empirical belief is a belief about the physical world resulting from sense experience or a belief about the "contents" of one's mind (one's thoughts, feelings, emotions, etc.) based on introspection (looking "inside"). A precise characterization of the distinction between empirical and non-empirical beliefs isn't possible without settling some of the controversies that will be discussed in this chapter and the next.

2   You will recall that the precise way of understanding this distinction is a matter of some controversy. Intuitively, the idea is that even when you are not

actually considering and assenting to a given claim (*occurrently* believing the claim) you might still believe the claim. All day yesterday, for example, you believed that 15 is greater than 1 though it is unlikely you actually considered the matter. We might say you dispositionally believe *P* when you would believe it were you to consider it. But as we saw that doesn't seem to distinguish between coming to believe *P* for the first time and having believed it all along.

3 On the standard interpretation of "or," if *P* is true then (*P* or *X*) is true for any *X* whatsoever.

4 For an argument that the charge of arbitrariness has more point that I am suggesting, see McGrew (1995, 13–17).

5 There is also a coherence theory of truth that might seem a natural ally of the coherence theory of justification. The problems facing a coherence theory of justification, however, pale in comparison to those facing the coherence theory of truth. See Fumerton (2002).

Chapter 4

Traditional (Internalist) Foundationalism

Introduction

The foundationalist is convinced that if we are to avoid the most radical of all skepticisms there must be a kind of justification for a belief that does not require the having of other justified beliefs. [The *existence* of non-inferential justification provides the solution to the threat of epistemic regress, and the *concept* of noninferential justification is employed in constructing the base clause in our recursive understanding of inferential justification.] But what could possibly constitute noninferential justification? If one can have an epistemically rational belief whose rationality is not even partially constituted by the having of other rational beliefs, what is the source of justification? What makes the belief rational?

There never was much of a consensus on how to understand noninferential justification, nor even on what beliefs are noninferentially justified. The epistemological landscape is even more difficult to map these days with the rise of internalism/externalism controversies concerning the nature of justification, controversies that we shall try to explain shortly. In this chapter, we will explore a number of "traditional" or "classical" accounts of noninferential justification. In the next chapter we will look at externalist accounts of noninferential justification. In chapter 6, we'll turn our attention to the way in which both internalists and externalists might approach an analysis of *inferential* justification.

Internalism/Externalism Controversies in Epistemology

I implied that traditional attempts to understand noninferential justification were internalist in nature. But what is this internalism/externalism controversy all about? The answer to that question is, unfortunately, more than a bit complicated. As is often the case in philosophy, technical terminology creeps into the discussion without a really clear understanding of what the terms mean. Furthermore, as the terms are used by different philosophers, their meaning evolves. By now, there are a number of importantly different controversies associated with the internalism/externalism debate. The debates are about the nature of justification, not just noninferential justification. But because we will be interested in understanding various views about the nature of noninferential justification in the context of the internalism/externalism controversy, it would be helpful to begin by defining that controversy as clearly as we can.

Internal state internalism

The most natural interpretation of the internalist's thesis about the nature of justification – one suggested by the very name for the view – is that the justification a person has for believing a proposition P at a time is constituted solely by the internal states of the person at that time. Of course, now we need an account of what is meant by "internal state." Often, both internalists and externalists rely on examples – [the internal states of a person include that person's subjective sense experiences, memories and beliefs,] for example. But that won't do. As we saw in chapter 2, as we ordinarily use most perceptual verbs ("see," "hear," "feel," etc.) and as we normally use the verb "to remember," the sentences employing them are factive. [You can't perceive a table without the table's existing (and perhaps causing the visual experience)]. Classical internalists don't want the table, or any state that includes the table as a constituent, to be part of an internal state of a subject. Unfortunately, it is not that easy to give a positive characterization of internal states that doesn't beg important questions concerning the nature of conscious beings.

If we are dualists (philosophers who think that the mind is distinct from the body), we might say that the internal states of a subject are the nonrelational properties of that subject's mind. A nonrelational property is a property whose exemplification never involves the existence of more than one thing.[1] So loving is a relational property, because John's loving

54

Mary is a state of affairs that involves as constituents both John and Mary. Being taller than is a relational property because John's being taller than Mary is a state of affairs that involves as constituents both John and Mary.

What are some uncontroversial examples of nonrelational properties? There really aren't any! It seems plausible enough to suppose that being red, or being round are good examples of nonrelational properties, but a glance at the history of philosophy will soon convince you that many philosophers think that a physical object's being red, for example, involves the exemplification of very complex relational properties. On one view, for example, being red is having the power to cause under certain conditions visual experiences of a certain sort. I think that being in pain is a — pain nonrelational property. But there are "behaviorists" who think that to be — objection in pain is to be disposed to behave in certain ways under certain conditions, and there are "functionalists" who think that to be in pain is to be in a state that plays a certain functional role in an organism.[2]

Are mental states internal states if we define internal states in terms of the exemplification of nonrelational properties? Traditional epistemologists have thought that they could carve out "narrow" mental states that satisfy the above definition. But that too has become a matter of considerable controversy. There is also an internalism/externalism controversy about the nature of many mental states. Most philosophers used to think that belief states, for example, are purely internal states. At the very least, such states don't involve the existence of anything in the physical world. These days, a great many philosophers of mind argue that one can't have certain beliefs unless one has interacted in various ways with the objects about which the belief is held. So, for example, some would argue that unless one has interacted directly or indirectly with physical objects, one can't even think about or form a belief about the physical world. On one crude view, the explanation for this alleged fact is simple. Belief states, and thoughts, represent reality, but the capacity to represent is itself a function of causal interaction. Just as a photograph is a photograph of Lincoln only if Lincoln was involved in the causal process that resulted in the print, so also, the argument goes, a thought (a "picture" in the mind) is a thought of X only if X was somehow or other involved in its production. The view as stated is far too crude and its scope will usually be quickly restricted to some sub class of beliefs – perhaps beliefs about simple propositions, things or properties. You can obviously believe that there are mermaids without your or anyone else's having run across such beings. But then the thought of a mermaid is in an intuitive sense *complex* – it involves the thought of a woman's head and torso, the tail of a fish, and so on.

Perhaps if we get down to the simplest of thoughts the externalist's view might seem more plausible.

This isn't a book on the philosophy of mind and I'm going to try to avoid as much as possible getting very involved in the internalism/externalism controversies concerning states like belief. I wanted to say only enough here to give you a feel for how the status of a mental state as "internal" can quickly become controversial. In any event, we do have one relatively clear understanding of internal states. The internal states of a person are those that involve only the exemplification by that person of nonrelational properties. It is an open question as to which states, if any, satisfy the definition.

Access internalism

These days internalism in epistemology is often more closely associated with access requirements for justification. The strongest version of the view argues that any conditions that constitute having justification for a belief must be conditions to which the believer has access. The access in question is usually construed not just as any knowledge or justified belief, but as introspective knowledge or justified belief. While the precise analysis of introspection is a matter of considerable controversy, the etymology of the word suggests that it is a kind of "looking" inward. Historically, introspective knowledge was construed as direct and immediate – something that requires no inference. So according to the strong access internalist, when S has justification for believing P, S knows directly and immediately that he has that justification. The idea behind access internalism is not, historically, unrelated to internal state internalism. For a great many historically important philosophers, being an internal state, being "in the mind," was closely associated with being the object of immediate introspective knowledge (though it is often not clear whether mental states were *defined* in terms of having this property or were viewed merely as states that have the property).

A slightly weaker version of access internalism insists only that when one has justification one is in a state to which one has potential, again usually potential *introspective*, access. There are as many different versions of potential access internalism (as we may call it) as there are different ways of understanding potentiality. So, one could insist that justification requires that it be *conceivable* that the person justified could discover that fact through introspection. Or one could insist that it must be *causally possible* for a person justified in believing P to discover that fact. Causal possibility itself can be understood in different ways. In one sense, it is

56

causally possible for me to dunk a basketball. It certainly doesn't violate any known laws of nature. On the other hand, there is a painfully clear sense in which I can't do it. A full description of my decrepit body, the Earth's gravitational mass, the details of my environment, and the laws of nature probably do preclude (or make exceedingly unlikely) that I rise above the rim.

One must be very careful lest (actual or potential) access internalism becomes unintelligible. If one maintains that for any set of conditions X that one proposes as *constitutive* of S's justification for believing P, those conditions must always be fortified with some other conditions describing S's access to X, then the view is hopeless. Regress once again rears its ugly head. Call the satisfaction of access conditions to X, $A1$. Will X together with $A1$ constitute justification for S to believe P? Not given this incautious statement of the view. Our strong access requirements require access (call that access $A2$) to the new proposed sufficient conditions for justification (X and $A1$). But the conjunction of X, $A1$, and $A2$ will not constitute S's justification for believing P either, as the view requires us to add access to these conditions, and so on *ad infinitum*. Given the view, we could in principle never come up with conditions that constitute justification.

To avoid this problem, the strong access internalist must distinguish carefully a view about what is *constitutive* of justification from a view about what is necessary for justification. If the view is to be intelligible, the access internalist must argue that when some set of conditions X constitutes S's justification for believing P, those conditions will be such that they entail that S has actual or potential access to them. The access, however, need not be part of what constitutes the justification. An analogy might be helpful. On any plausible view, P cannot be true unless it is true that P is true – P's truth entails (in some sense of "entails") that it is true that P is true. But it would be a serious mistake to argue that P's being true is constituted by (the more complex fact of) its being true that P is true. The correct analysis of what it is for P to be true should not make reference to truths about P's truth, even if the correct analysis of P's being true must reveal why P couldn't be true without its also being true that P is true.

Still, even if one can embrace access requirements and avoid conceptual regress, one might be caught in a dilemma. If the possibility in question is anything other than logical possibility (where a plausible test of such possibility is conceivability) it seems unlikely that most people could satisfy access requirements. In order to have justification for believing P, I would need to be able to access that justification, access the fact that

I've got access to that justification, and so on *ad infinitum.* Speaking for myself, I don't think I can keep things straight for more than two or three levels of increasingly complex acts of awareness. If, on the other hand, we insist only on the conceivability of access, it is not clear that the access requirements have much bite. A God-like being might have direct access to all sorts of conditions, and it is not clear that there is any contradiction in supposing that I could at any time evolve into a God-like being.

Inferential internalism

I indicated earlier that the second clause of the principle of inferential justification is highly controversial. It is a clause rejected by almost all paradigm externalists and it will be useful later on to define *inferential internalists* as those who accept the principle that to be justified in believing *P* on the basis of *E* one must be justified in believing that *E* makes probable *P*. *Inferential externalists* are those who reject this clause of the principle. Notice, however, that one can embrace inferential internalism – the idea that in order to legitimately infer *P* from *E* one must have reason to believe that there is an appropriate connection between *E* and *P* – without accepting the superficially similar access requirements for justification. An inferential internalist need not hold that in order to have justification for believing *P* one must be in a position to access (introspectively or in any other way) the fact that one has such justification. The inferential internalist insists only that there must be access to evidential connections (relations of making probable or entailment between one's evidence and one's conclusion) for inferences to yield justification.

Internalism and nonnaturalism

I have argued elsewhere (1995, chapter 3) that in the end the internalism/externalism debate might hinge on the issue of what concepts philosophers in the respective camps employ in their attempt to explain both noninferential and inferential justification. Put far too crudely, externalists seek to identify being justified with the exemplification of so-called *natural* properties, while internalists reject the "naturalization" of epistemology. What's a natural property? Well, you should probably ask a self-proclaimed naturalist. As far as *I* can tell, the natural properties are those that are "scientifically respectable." They certainly include any of the properties referred to in the formulation of physical laws and also *nomological* properties – properties defined in terms of causation or lawful connection. As we'll see, most externalists lean heavily on our under-

58

standing of causal or lawful connection in their attempt to say what constitutes the having of a justified belief.

Traditional (Internalist?) Analyses of Noninferential Justification

I spent some time trying to sketch at least an outline of the internalism/externalism controversies concerning the nature of justification. I haven't offered much by way of argument for or against various positions, though I have warned of the threat of regress posed by access internalism. I now want to return to the question of how to understand noninferential justification. I'll begin with a survey of what I take to be classic analyses. In the course of evaluating those analyses we can attempt to determine in what senses, if any, they are internalist. In the next chapter, we'll look at more recent self-proclaimed externalist accounts of noninferential justification.

Noninferential justification and infallible belief

In our discussion of knowledge we looked at strong Cartesian requirements for knowledge. Descartes could just as easily be construed as proposing criteria for finding appropriate *foundations* for knowledge – the metaphor of foundations is one that he himself employed. We have changed the topic from knowledge to justification, but in looking for the foundations of *justification* we may also find the foundations for *knowledge*. This is precisely what one would expect if the key element in acquiring noninferential knowledge is acquiring noninferential justification.

While most epistemologists were quick to give up infallibility as the mark of knowledge in general, *traditional* foundationalists often seemed to either explicitly or implicitly endorse the view that we have found noninferentially justified beliefs when we have found beliefs that cannot be mistaken – when we have found, that is, infallible beliefs. But how, precisely, shall we understand the concept of an infallible belief? Following Lehrer (1974), we might suggest the following:

S's belief that *P* is infallible when *S*'s believing that *P* entails[3] that *P* is true.

To see truth-tracking in notes.

There do appear to be beliefs that satisfy the definition. As Descartes famously observed, my believing that I exist entails that I do exist. My believing that I have beliefs entails that someone has beliefs. By contrast, my believing that there are mermaids does not entail that there are mermaids. But while the above definition of infallible belief is perfectly clear, it is not at all obvious that it will be of much use to the *epistemologist* trying to understand foundational justification. As Lehrer pointed out, it is trivially true that a necessary truth is entailed by every proposition. Remember that P entails Q when it is impossible for P to be true while Q is false. But if Q is a necessary truth (say, $2 + 2 = 4$), it is (trivially) impossible for Q to be false, and thus impossible for anything else to be true while Q is false. But then my believing Q (again trivially) entails that Q is true when Q is a necessary truth. If I believe a necessary truth, I have an infallible belief. But suppose I believe some very complicated necessary truth N because my fortune teller told me that N is true. I couldn't for the life of me recognize N as a necessary truth, nor would I even accept it as a truth were it not for the advice I got from my seer. Surely no-one would think that I had any sort of good justification, let alone noninferential justification, for believing N.

To deal with the problem, one could suggest that infallible belief constitutes noninferential justification only if the proposition believed is not necessary. That won't work either. Consider again my belief that someone has beliefs. That belief is infallible. The fact that I have the belief entails that it is true. But the proposition that someone has beliefs entails the following proposition: (P) If someone has beliefs then either it is the case that snow is both white and not white or someone has beliefs. P might be a bit too complicated for me to understand fully, but again I might believe it on the basis of my notoriously unreliable fortune teller. Once again I will have an unjustified but infallible belief.

There are many ways of tinkering with the definition of infallible belief to avoid these sorts of objections to the suggestion that we identify noninferential justification with infallible belief. But once one sees that the *mere* entailment holding between the having of a belief and the belief's being true, *an entailment which one might be quite incapable of discovering*, hardly generates justification, one might begin to suspect that we are on the wrong track in our search for a plausible account of noninferential justification. This conclusion might be reinforced if we look at some of the other most plausible candidates for noninferentially justified belief. Consider, for example, the justification I have for believing that I am in pain shortly after banging my knee against the car door. Most *traditional* foundationalists have thought that the justification in question is both noninferential and about as good as justification can get. But is it plausible to suppose that my belief that I am in pain entails that I am in pain? It's hard to see how it can. Isn't it at least possible that the brain state

60

causally responsible for my belief that I am in pain is simply a different brain state than the brain state causally responsible for my pain? If it were then it ought to be possible to produce the belief without its truth-maker. To be sure, the argument is far from conclusive. I suppose one might argue that if one thinks carefully about the belief one will see that it literally *contains* the pain as a constituent – it is "directed at" the pain in such a way that the pain must exist in order for the belief to exist. If you had enough nerve, you might saunter into the department of neurophysiology to assure the cognitive scientists that you had an ironclad philosophical argument proving that whatever brain state produces belief about one's pain simply must contain as a constituent a brain state that produces pain. One worries, however, that the neurophysiologist has every reason to be skeptical of such *a priori* neurophysiology, and if that's right, we really aren't in a position to claim that the belief that one is in pain entails that the pain exists. But is that really a reason to reject the belief as one that can be noninferentially justified?

Noninferential justification as infallible justification

Whatever one thinks of the above rather abstract argument, I do want to suggest that it was always a bit odd to think that one could find noninferential justification in the mere having of a belief that somehow guarantees its own truth. Indeed, I don't think that even Descartes was interested in that sort of infallibility. Noninferential justification *might* bring with it infallibility, but if it does it is the possession of the *justification* that guarantees the truth of what is believed. It is not the mere fact that I *believe* that I'm in pain that justifies me in believing that I am in pain. Surely, we want to bring the *pain* itself into the picture as a constituent of the justification. But how are we going to do that?

The simplest approach would be to construe the pain as the justifier. The answer to the question of what justifies me in believing that I am in pain is that it is the very pain that makes true what I believe. The justification is noninferential because it does not involve the having of other justified beliefs. It is constituted instead by the feature of the world that makes true what I believe. But are we really making progress? What precisely is it about this pain that makes it a justifier of *my* belief that I'm in pain, but doesn't make it a justifier of *your* belief that I'm in pain. When you believe that Paris is in France, your belief might be justified, but the traditional foundationalist is not going to allow that one can identify Paris's being in France as the noninferential justifier for the belief. But what's the difference between my being in pain and Paris's being in

France, the difference that makes it appropriate to identify the former as a justification for me to believe that I'm in pain, while the latter is no justification at all for my belief about a city in France?

Following Russell and others, it seems to me that we should look for noninferential justification not in the truth maker (the fact that makes true the belief) *by itself*, but in a *relation* that the believer bears to the truth maker. It is the fact that I have a kind of direct access, awareness, or acquaintance with the pain, an access that I do not have to Paris, that gives me noninferential justification for believing that I am in pain.

Acquaintance and noninferential justification

I have argued that neither a belief nor the fact that makes true what is believed is by itself a plausible justification, let alone the kind of justification that might end a regress of justification. Rather, we must stand in some sort of special relation to the truth of what is believed, or more precisely, we must stand in some sort of special relation to the *fact* that makes true what we believe. Again, following Russell, I have argued elsewhere (1995) that the most fundamental concept required to make sense of traditional foundationalism is the concept of direct acquaintance with a fact. Unfortunately, one cannot develop such a view in a philosophical vacuum. There are a host of controversial presuppositions the view requires, presuppositions that take us far beyond the scope of this book. Let me, however, briefly sketch some of the background assumptions that I bring to this account of noninferential justification, recognizing that there may well be plausible variations on these consistent with the general spirit of a foundationalism based on direct acquaintance.

I take the primary bearers of truth-value to be thoughts (which I also refer to as "propositions"). We do, of course, also refer to sentences (written and uttered) as true or false. On this view, however, their truth value is *derivative*. A sentence is true when it expresses a thought that is true. On the *highly* controversial view in philosophy of mind that I accept, thoughts are non-relational properties of a mind or self. True thoughts correspond to or "picture" facts (features of reality). False thoughts fail to correspond. A fact is a non-linguistic complex that consists of a thing's or things' exemplifying properties (e.g. this table's being brown or this table's being next to that chair). The world contained facts long before it contained minds and thoughts. However, in one perfectly clear sense the world might have contained no *truths* before there were conscious beings, for without conscious beings there would be no bearers of truth value.[4]

62

On the view I defend, [*intentional* states – mental states that appear to have objects (the belief *that P*, the desire *that P*, the fear *that P*, etc.) – are species of thought.] Believing that there are ghosts and fearing that there are ghosts are species of the thought that there are ghosts. The belief that there are ghosts is true when the thought that there are ghosts corresponds to the fact that there are ghosts. In fact, that belief is false, because it fails to correspond to any such fact.

On a classic acquaintance theory of noninferential justification, one has [noninferential justification for believing *P* when one has the thought that *P* while one is directly acquainted with the thought's corresponding to the fact that *P*.] But what is this all-important relation of acquaintance? The answer might be disappointing. Again, on the classic view, [acquaintance is *sui generis*, an unanalyzable relation that holds between a person and a thing, a property, or a fact.] To be sure, one can invoke metaphors. So it is sometimes said that [when you are acquainted with a fact (say your pain), there is nothing standing "between" you and the fact. The fact is simply "there" before consciousness.] But spatial metaphors are bound to mislead. [Facts with which one is acquainted are spatially no "nearer" to the person acquainted with them than facts with which one is not acquainted.]

To say that the relation of acquaintance is *sui generis* and unanalyzable is to emphasize that it is unlike any other relation and that it defies analysis. In our earlier discussion of Williamson's views about knowledge, we emphasized that there must be conceptual building blocks if we are to have any understanding at all. While I was not terribly sympathetic to the view that we can't say anything interesting about the constituents of knowledge in general, I do think that the key to understanding *noninferential* justification/knowledge is our understanding of an unanalyzable relation of direct acquaintance.

The difficulty with introducing [a concept as primitive (indefinable) is that other philosophers will often claim to have no idea] what you are talking about. As philosophers, we'd like to avoid "stand offs" of this sort ("Well I know what I'm talking about," I say. "Well I don't," my critic says). One *can* certainly attempt to "ostend" (point to) that which one cannot define. The paradigm of an ostensive definition involves physically pointing to a kind of thing, but there are other ways of directing someone's attention. It is not obvious to me, for example, that I can offer an analysis or definition of pain. But I can kick you hard and ask you if you noticed any dramatic change in your mental life. Having given you the concept of pain in this way, I might *also* try to get you to reflect on the awareness you have of your pain. Like most relations, however, it is a

63

bit hard to focus your attention just on the relation. (Try, for example, to form an idea of being taller than without thinking of a pair of things standing in that relation.) Still, I might ask you to think about situations in which you were[aware of an intense pain, got lost in an engaging conversation, and for a while no longer *noticed* the pain.]There are two main reactions philosophers have to the thought experiment. One is to hold [that in such situations the pain itself temporarily ceased. The other, however, is to hold that the pain continued, though for awhile you were no longer aware of it. If one *can* make sense of the latter, then one can isolate direct acquaintance. Direct acquaintance is the relation you were in to the pain before you got lost in conversation, which ceased during the conversation, and which came into existence again as the conversation ended.]

One can also try to "point" to acquaintance by giving examples of the [facts with which one is acquainted and contrasting those facts with others of which one can become aware only through inference.] Unfortunately, as we shall see in our examination of skeptical arguments, even acquaintance theorists might not agree with each other when it comes to identifying the objects of acquaintance.

Just as one might like an analysis of acquaintance, one might also expect an analysis of a thought's corresponding to a fact – the complex fact acquaintance with which yields noninferential justification. Again, disappointment awaits. Correspondence is sometimes thought of as a picturing relation, but the picturing metaphor is largely responsible for caricatures of the view. It is tempting to at least mention the metaphor of a Kodak print and the scene it depicts as a way of explaining the relation that true thought bears to the fact with which it corresponds. But most thoughts are not literally pictures and the relation of correspondence certainly has nothing to do with any kind of similarity that holds between the thought and the fact it represents. Correspondence is not like anything else, and it cannot be analyzed into any less problematic concepts.[5]

The attempt to understand noninferential justification in terms of direct acquaintance with facts has come under relentless criticism. We have already noted that many reject the intelligibility of both acquaintance and a relation of correspondence between thoughts and facts. These days, facts themselves are not philosophically unproblematic. Many philosophers think that reference to facts is just a disguised way of talking about truths. Still others argue that even if we could make sense of acquaintance, it wouldn't do us any good in our search for foundations of *knowledge* and *justification*. In one of the most influential arguments against foundationalism, Sellars (1963) argued that the idea of acquaintance with reality

Sellars

– also often referred to as reality's being directly *given* to one – contains irreconcilable tensions. On the one hand, to ensure that something's being given does not involve any other beliefs, proponents of the view want direct acquaintance to be untainted by the application of concepts or thought. The kinds of data with which we are acquainted are presumably given in sense experience to all sorts of other creatures, many of which lack concepts altogether. On the other hand, the whole doctrine of the given is designed to end a regress of justification, to give us secure foundations for the rest of what we justifiably *infer* from the given. But to make intelligible the idea of an inference from the given, the given would have to be propositional – it would have to be the kind of thing that is true or false, the kind of thing that could serve as a *premise* in an argument. But one generates the bearers of truth value only through the application of concepts or thought.

A solution to the dilemma presented by Sellars (and others) is to emphasize that direct acquaintance is not *by itself* an epistemic relation. Acquaintance is a relation that other animals probably bear to properties and even facts, but it also probably does not give these animals any kind of justification for believing anything, precisely because these other animals probably do not have beliefs. Without thought there is no truth, and without a bearer of truth-value there is nothing to be justified or unjustified. But how does acquaintance yield noninferential justification? The suggestion, again, is that one has noninferential justification for believing *P* when one has the thought that *P and* when one is acquainted with the correspondence between the thought that *P* and the fact that *P*. The idea is that when one has immediately before consciousness both the truth bearer and the truth maker one has all one needs, all one could ever want, by way of justification.

Is noninferential justification, understood this way, infallible justification, i.e. justification that precludes the possibility of error? It obviously is. When one is directly acquainted with the feature of the world that makes one's belief true, one's belief is true. One can't stand in a real relation to the fact that *P* without the thought that *P* being true. When I am directly acquainted with my pain – when the pain is immediately before consciousness – my belief that I am in pain must be true. The "picture" and what it pictures are all immediately present to my mind.[6]

It is sometimes argued that once thought enters the picture infallibility disappears. There certainly are views about the nature of thought that make it difficult for one to reconcile the application of concepts with the impossibility of error. So one might think that to categorize something as pain is to compare that thing with some past paradigm of a painful experience, or to make a judgment about what the linguistic community would *say* in describing the thing. If a view like either of these were true then it would hardly be plausible to suppose that one couldn't make a mistake in judging that one is in pain. But that's because if either view were true, being in pain would be the kind of state (being similar to that paradigm, or being the subject of certain descriptions) with which one has no acquaintance. The obvious response to any such view is to deny the account of concept application it presupposes.

Acquaintance and a priori *justification*

I said earlier that even philosophers sympathetic with the idea of grounding noninferential justification on direct acquaintance with facts disagree with each other when it comes to identifying the objects of acquaintance. I often use pain as the paradigm of a state with which one can be directly acquainted, and most acquaintance theorists have thought that certain sorts of mental states are among the best examples of facts with which one can be acquainted in such a way as to generate noninferential justification. The other favorite example of foundationally justified belief, however, is belief in at least simple *necessary* truths (e.g. that $2 + 2 = 4$, that triangles have three sides, that everything that is red is colored). Can acquaintance theorists accommodate these given the account of non-inferential justification they defend?

They certainly think that they can. The key is to find the relevant truth makers for necessary truths and to argue that one can be acquainted with them. Although the terminology was not always the same, the traditional epistemologist recognized a distinction between *a posteriori* knowledge/justification and *a priori* knowledge/justification. As a first stab, *a priori* knowledge is knowledge that is independent of experience. *A posteriori* knowledge is knowledge that rests on experience. But this obviously requires immediate clarification. *A priori* knowledge is not knowledge independent of any experience whatsoever. The paradigm of *a posteriori* knowledge is knowledge that rests on *sense* experience. You know that there is a tree outside your window on the basis of visual sense experience. You know that the turkey is almost cooked on the basis of olfactory sense experience. The *a posteriori* was almost always extended to include introspective knowledge – knowledge you get by "looking" inside yourself to find such mental states as pain, belief, fear, desire, etc. You don't need sense experience to justify your belief that $2 + 2 = 4$, or that triangles have three sides. Of course you do need experience of some sort or another. Beings who are literally unconscious have no knowledge of anything. The idea seemed to be, however, that if one simply thought carefully enough about the proposition that $2 + 2 = 4$ or the proposition that triangles have three sides one could come to see the truth of those propositions. To be sure, one might never have acquired the idea of two or the idea of being a triangle without sense experience. And most of us remember that it probably helped to have our first-grade teachers manipulate some apples on the desk in an effort to give us the basic idea of addition. But having acquired the relevant concepts, we are now able to simply "see" with the "mind's eye" the truth of various propositions that employ those concepts.

On the *traditional* view, the paradigms of truths one could discover without relying on the senses were necessary truths.[7] A necessary truth is one that doesn't just happen to be true, but which *must* be true. If a truth is necessary there is no *possible* world, no *possible* circumstance in which it is false. Necessary truths are also sometimes described as truths whose falsehood is quite *inconceivable*. Unfortunately, all of these characterizations of necessary truth are problematic as attempts to illuminate the concept of necessity, because they all implicitly presuppose an understanding of it. A proposition is necessarily true if it must be true. But the "must" is just another way of talking about the necessity. A truth is necessary if there is no possible world in which it is false. But a world, or better a complex description, is possible only if its denial is not necessary. If a truth is necessary its falsehood is inconceivable. But a falsehood is inconceivable if it is impossible to conceive of that falsehood. It is impossible to conceive of a falsehood when it is a necessary truth that one doesn't conceive of the falsehood.

More informative accounts of necessary truths are all highly controversial. So one sort of necessary truth is called "analytic." It is necessarily and analytically true that bachelors are unmarried, on one view, because the very idea or concept of being a bachelor contains the idea or concept of being unmarried. On a more linguistic characterization, the sentence "Bachelors are unmarried" expresses an analytic truth because the meaning of "bachelor" includes the meaning of "unmarried."

Although he didn't use the term "necessary truth," David Hume (1888, e.g., p. 458) distinguished truths that depend on the way in which our ideas correspond to *matters of fact*, from truths that depend only on relations between ideas. The latter certainly included the analytic truths, but arguably included many more truths as well. Consider, for example, the truth that being red is different from being blue. On Hume's view, one could discover that truth simply by reflecting on the fact that the idea of being red is a different idea from the idea of being blue. It is not at all clear, however, that the idea of being red is constituted in whole or in part by the idea of being different from blue. It seems plausible to suppose that someone might have the idea of being red without ever having acquired the concept of blue. On Hume's view it is not all that clear that we should draw a sharp line between introspective knowledge of pain, and knowledge of the truth that triangles have three sides. In both cases one looks "within" to find the respective truth makers. In coming to know that one is in pain one finds "within" the pain itself. In coming to know that triangles have three sides, one finds "within" ideas bearing certain relations to one another.

While Hume tried to ground necessary truth in relations between ideas, others were more comfortable finding the truth makers for necessary truths in relations between *properties*, where often properties were thought of as entities whose existence is quite independent of their being exemplified by anything – entities that are either outside of space and time, or that are in any event eternal.[8] On this view, what makes it true that triangles have three sides is the fact that the property of being a triangle (a property which might have existed without anyone's thinking of it) contains the property of having three sides). What makes it true that being red is different from being blue is that the properties referred to (being red and being blue) are indeed different. But they don't just happen to be different. The property of being a triangle couldn't possibly exist without "containing" the property of having three sides, and the properties of being red and being blue couldn't exist without being different from one another.

Earlier, I pointed out that on Hume's view of the truth makers for necessary truths, there isn't all that much difference between the way in which one discovers certain contingent facts about one's mental life and the way in which one discovers necessary truths. Both involve "looking" within. On an acquaintance theory of noninferential justification, there is, similarly, a common source of both noninferential *a posteriori* knowledge and noninferential *a priori* knowledge. That source, of course, is acquaintance. Just as one can be directly acquainted with pain, so also one can be directly acquainted with ideas and their relations. Plato, Russell, and countless others also thought that one can become acquainted "through thought" with properties and the relations they bear to other properties. So whether one thinks that it is relations between ideas or relations between properties that are the truth makers for necessary truths, one could discover the truth of a necessary truth by being acquainted with the relevant truth makers (while one has the thought that represents those truth makers).

One might worry that an acquaintance theory is collapsing the critical epistemological distinction between two radically different sorts of knowledge – the *a priori* and the *a posteriori* – but the proponent of the view might very well claim that it is an advantage of an acquaintance theory that one can offer a *unified* account of both types of noninferential knowledge. Whether one knows noninferentially a contingent fact about one's mental life or one knows noninferentially a necessary truth, it is direct acquaintance with a truth maker that is the critical component of that knowledge.

Traditional foundationalism and internal state internalism

We distinguished a number of different traditional versions of foundationalism. These views are sometimes thought of as versions of internalism about justification, but it might be useful to pause and consider in what senses, if any, these traditional views really are versions of internalism, at least about noninferential justification. The view that identifies a noninferentially justified belief with an infallible belief might certainly be viewed as a version of internal state internalism. After all, on the most natural reading of the view, it is an internal state – a belief – that is the justifier. But in our brief discussion of candidates for internal states we had occasion to note that some philosophers of mind reject the hypothesis that the constituents of a belief state are all internal to the believer. There are all sorts of different reasons offered in support of such a view. But consider a relatively straightforward consideration. At least some would argue that in perception we can form what is sometimes called a *de re* belief. A *de re* belief is a belief about a thing – the very subject of the belief is literally a constituent of it. When I'm looking at a particular dog and believe of it that it is hungry, some would argue that the dog itself has entered into the belief state. I couldn't have that belief (though I could have one like it) were the animal not present. If a view like that were true, then having the belief that the dog exists might literally entail the dog's existence. Of course, one needs an account of the conditions under which one can bring the object of a belief "into" the belief state. On one traditional view acquaintance again plays a pivotal role. The only objects that can enter into belief states, some philosophers would argue, are objects with which we are directly acquainted. For reasons we will discuss later, many of these same philosophers were convinced that we are never directly acquainted with anything in the physical world (or the past, or the future). Others, sometimes called direct realists, have thought that one can be directly aware of physical objects, or at least constituents of physical objects, and thus have held that even if a belief can contain only those objects with which we are acquainted a belief can sometimes include as a constituent an external object.

The idea that only objects with which we are acquainted can be literal constituents of belief states is itself not very popular today – no more popular than the foundationalism built around the concept of direct acquaintance. As we noted earlier, it is often the case that contemporary philosophers of mind take the identity conditions for a belief state (the conditions that make the belief the belief that it is) to involve factors causally critical to the formation of the state that becomes a belief. Any such view seems to imply that beliefs are literally constituted by factors external to the believer. All of this is a reminder that even if we locate noninferential justifiers in belief states, it is not obvious that we will have located noninferential justification in an exclusively internal state of the believer.

It is also important to realize that strictly speaking, according to the "infallibilist," it is the property of being infallible that makes the belief a justifier. That property is relational. A belief is infallible when its occurrence entails its truth. It is not clear that all of the constituents of the complex state of affairs which is a belief's entailing its truth are internal to the believer. A great deal depends on how one understands entailment and its relata. On at least one view, a belief's entailing its truth would involve a relation between the believing and a proposition, and, again on some views, propositions (the most fundamental bearers of truth and falsehood) are not mental entities. Again, it becomes unclear as to whether the view that identifies foundational justification with a belief's being infallible is a version of internal state internalism.

Most of what was said about infallible belief and internal states applies also to the acquaintance theory of noninferential justification. Acquaintance is a relation. My being acquainted with a fact is only straightforwardly an internal state of me when the fact with which I am acquainted is constituted solely by my internal states. But the metaepistemological view that acquaintance is the source of noninferential justification leaves open the question of what can be an object of direct acquaintance. Again, on the classic model, the paradigms of states with which you can be acquainted were your internal mental states – sensations like pain, for example. But it is at least an open question, one we will debate later, as to whether one can be directly acquainted with external objects.

As we also saw in our brief discussion of *a priori* justification, at least some acquaintance theorists want to ground *a priori* justification in the possibility of being directly acquainted with properties and their relations. Again, it is not at all obvious that the properties with which you are acquainted in thought are constituents of your "inner" mental life. If one can be directly acquainted with properties and their relations, and properties have an existence which is external to the mind, then the complex state of affairs which is one's being directly acquainted with a property is not unproblematically an internal state. If it can partially constitute non-inferential justification, then it is also not unproblematic to identify this sort of noninferential justification with an internal state.

Lastly, as we emphasized in responding to the objection Sellars raises to the doctrine of the given, the most plausible candidate for the source of noninferential justification might be direct acquaintance with the complex fact which is a thought's (belief's) corresponding to a fact. Everything said about the controversial character of belief as an internal state would render controversial the claim that acquaintance with a belief is an internal state.

Traditional foundationalism and access internalism

While internalism is sometimes defined in terms of its commitment to the view that the justification one has for a belief is a function of one's internal states, it is also closely associated with the view that if one has justification for believing some proposition *P*, one must be able to discover that fact through careful reflection. In characterizing that view, we noted that there are as many different versions of the view as there are interpretations of the "ability" in question. Certainly, if ability is interpreted robustly, it seems unlikely that just because a belief is infallible, the believer would have the ability to recognize it as such. That, in effect, was one obvious problem the view faced. We had no difficulty imagining situations in which someone had a belief that was infallible even though there wasn't the slightest chance that the person could actually discover that fact. In such situations, it is difficult to see how the infallibility of a belief was epistemically relevant. Of course, the moral one might draw from thinking about this objection to infallibility as the locus of foundations is that one must respect the insight of access internalism. On the other hand, we also worried that access internalism would require too much of non-inferential justification – that it would generate a vicious regress.

If there is such a thing as direct acquaintance with facts and the correspondence that holds between thought and such facts, could one accommodate the demands of the access internalist – at least with respect to noninferential justification? When one is directly acquainted with one's pain does it follow that one either is, or could easily become, directly acquainted with the fact that one is directly acquainted with that pain? If one thinks only about moving "up one level," one might suppose that the prospects aren't that bad. Indeed, if asked why I believe that there is such a thing as direct acquaintance with a fact, I might very well suggest that I find myself directly acquainted with direct acquaintance! While the answer will no doubt leave my critic unhappy, it would be unreasonable to expect any other answer. If the foundationalism grounded in acquaintance is a true view, why would it be reasonable to forbid the proponent of the view from locating key elements in the source of its justification through direct acquaintance? Still, if the view is that whenever one possesses justification for believing any proposition whatsoever, one must always be able to introspectively access the justification one possesses, one must surely be wary before accepting the regress such a view generates. I might be acquainted with the fact that I'm acquainted with pain. And I might even be acquainted with the fact that I'm acquainted with the fact that I'm acquainted with the fact that I'm in pain. But I'm not at all sure I can generate infinitely many ever increasingly complex acts of acquaintance. At some level, then, it seems that I might have a noninferentially justified belief without having the capacity to access (noninferentially) the fact that I've got a noninferentially justified belief.

Still, one might argue, if I get confused at higher levels, it is merely due to contingent features of my finite intellect. There would be nothing in principle to prevent me from possessing infinitely many levels of noninferentially justified belief about lower level noninferential justification. But if the access internalist is retreating to the logical possibility of access, it is not clear that even the externalist has any difficulties meeting access requirements. This is a point to which we shall return in the next chapter.

Noninferential justification and the rejection of naturalistic epistemology

If there is a relatively clear sense in which the acquaintance theory is anathema to externalist epistemologies, it is in its reliance on the *sui generis* "nonnatural" relation of acquaintance. As I indicated earlier, paradigm externalists endorse a naturalistic approach to understanding key epistemic concepts. In particular, as we shall see, the epistemic status of a belief is usually viewed as a function of the belief's causal history or its causal sensitivity to the environment. If natural properties are those that feature in the explanations and descriptions of phenomena offered by natural science, direct acquaintance is a poor candidate for a natural property. Of

72

course, if one has a broader understanding of natural properties, all bets are off when it comes to characterizing a given property or relation as natural or nonnatural. The direct acquaintance theorist is convinced that there is such a relation as acquaintance, and facts about what people are directly acquainted with are as much a part of the "furniture" of the world as are facts about the molecular composition of water.[9]

Suggested readings

BonJour, Laurence and Sosa, Ernest. 2003. *Epistemic Justification*, part I. Oxford: Blackwell.

Fales, Evan. 1996. *A Defense of the Given*, chapters 1 and 6. Lanham, MD: Rowman and Littlefield.

Russell, Bertrand. 1959. *The Problems of Philosophy*, chapter 5. Oxford: Oxford University Press.

Notes

1   One needs the "never constituted" because it might be true that the exemplification of some relational properties *need* not involve more than one entity. I know people who love themselves. Loving is still a relational property even if its exemplification by a narcissist requires the existence only of the narcissist. That is so because loving is sometimes exemplified by a pair of things, as when John loves Mary.

2   So a really crude functionalist might suggest that to be in pain is to be in that state that results from some sort of damage to the body and in turn leads to behavior that is conducive to the avoidance of further damage.

3   We can distinguish different sorts of entailment. When we speak of one proposition P entailing another Q we are always in some sense describing the fact that P's being true would guarantee that Q is true. But some entailments hold (or can be recognized) solely in virtue of the form of the propositions standing in that relation (e.g. that it is raining entails that it is either raining or snowing). Call these formal entailments. Others can be recognized only by reflecting on the meaning or the content of the propositions in question (e.g. that there are bachelors entails that there are men who are unmarried). When these can be reduced to formal entailments through the substitution of synonymous expressions we might call these analytic entailments. Some philosophers would also recognize synthetic entailments. P synthetically entails Q when it is absolutely impossible that P be true while Q is false but one can't reduce the necessary connection to formal entailment through substitution of synonymous expressions. There are no uncontroversial examples, but the

following is as promising as any: That there are red things entails that there are things that are not blue all over. In this discussion I want entailment to be understood broadly enough to include formal, analytic, and synthetic entailment.

4 The truth about truth is more complicated than this. See Fumerton (2002) for a more complete defense of this sort of view.

5 Again, all of this is highly controversial. There are no shortages of attempts to define the relation that holds between thoughts and what they represent. Some focus on causal connections, for example, as the key to understanding representation or correspondence – the thought of X is the state of an individual caused in the appropriate way by X – at least in the case of simple thoughts. A great deal is built into the qualification "in the appropriate way."

6 An acquaintance theorist might allow that one can be noninferentially justified in believing the false proposition that P in virtue of being directly acquainted with a fact that is very much like, but not quite identical with, the fact that is the truth maker for P.

7 These days, matters are considerably more complicated. Largely, due to the work of Saul Kripke (1980) many, if not most, contemporary philosophers believe that one can have *a priori* knowledge of contingent truths and that there are necessary truths that can be known only *a posteriori*. To explore even superficially this view we would need to make an extensive tour of highly complex controversies in the philosophy of language, the nature of essential properties, the nature of reference, and the status of identity claims. I have argued elsewhere (1989) that the pivotal assumptions on which Kripke-style arguments rest are confused, but here I can only alert the reader that there is heated debate over whether or not one should reject traditional views over what can and can't be known *a priori*.

8 Why would anyone think this? Debate over the status of properties has a very long history. In fact, it may be that their status as eternal beings was attractive to some philosophers precisely because they were searching for a truth-maker for a kind of truth that seemed necessary.

9 For an excellent defense of this general line of thought, see Richard Feldman's "We are All Naturalists Now."

Chapter 5

Externalist Versions of Foundationalism

Introduction

In the last chapter we surveyed some of the more traditional versions of foundationalism, views often associated with internalism. I developed in some detail the account of noninferential justification I take to be the most plausible. That account ends the epistemic and conceptual regress of justification with the concept of direct acquaintance, a concept that is *sui generis*, that cannot be reduced to any more fundamental concepts. I tried to make clear the sense in which a foundationalism grounded in direct acquaintance satisfies the various descriptions of internalism, noting that it is not at all obvious that the view, however traditional it might be, is committed to either internal state internalism or internalism understood in terms of robust access requirements. We haven't talked at all about how a direct acquaintance theorist might propose that we move beyond foundationally justified belief to acquire inferential justification. That is a project that we will address in chapter 6.

It is an understatement to suggest that the kind of foundationalism I described in the last chapter is no longer the received view in epistemology. Although I can't convince you of it here, I do think some version of the acquaintance theory was at least implicitly supposed by the vast majority of philosophers over a couple of thousand years of thinking about knowledge. Foundationalism itself has made a significant comeback in recent years, but in a quite different form. Externalists end epistemic and conceptual regresses with a quite different understanding of noninferential justification.

Externalism

The most influential epistemologist in the last twenty-five years has been Alvin Goldman. If a philosopher's importance is to be measured by the effect that philosopher has on the field, Goldman's contribution to epistemology can hardly be overstated. Although Quine is often credited as the first philosopher to clearly recommend "naturalizing" epistemology, it is Goldman who tried to develop in a systematic way an understanding of critical epistemic concepts that would allow one to make sense of Quine's suggestion that we study knowledge and justification "scientifically." In fact, over the years Goldman and others influenced by him made a number of importantly different suggestions for how to understand knowledge and justified belief, each of which carried with it, explicitly or implicitly, a view about how to understand *foundational* knowledge and justified belief.

Goldman's early causal theory

In an early response to Gettier counterexamples to the justified true belief account of knowledge, Goldman (1967) proposed a *causal* theory of knowledge. Thinking about what some Gettier counterexamples seem to have in common, Goldman speculated that what prevented knowledge in Gettier situations was the lack of a causal connection between the truth maker of a belief and the belief. So in Russell's example of the person looking at the broken clock and by sheer luck reaching a true conclusion about the time of day, the fact that made true the belief was not causally efficacious in producing the belief. When I believe the disjunction (*P* or *Q*) based on the justified but false belief that *P*, the actual truth maker (*Q*) for the disjunction is not part of what caused me to believe (*P* or *Q*). It's certainly not clear that *all* Gettier counterexamples should be diagnosed as featuring the absence of a causal connection between truth maker and belief. In the land of fake barns, you will recall, it was the existence of a real barn that caused the person to believe that the barn was there. But there were enough examples in which there appeared to be a missing causal link to suggest to Goldman the causal theory of knowing.

The crudest version of the theory takes knowledge to be a true belief caused by the fact that makes true the belief. To accommodate the possibility of knowing truths about the future, Goldman suggested amending the theory to allow as knowledge true belief caused by a fact that causes the truth-maker for the belief. To avoid counterexamples involving "deviant" causal chains, Goldman further qualified the view to suggest that the causal connections sufficient for knowledge be roughly along the lines envisioned by the believer. So a mad neurophysiologist controlling my brain might have been inspired by a past experience of the mountain outside my window to induce in me an hallucinatory experience that leads me to believe truly that there is a mountain outside my window. While the belief might be true and caused in a roundabout way by the very mountain that makes true my belief, the belief didn't come about in the *way* I took for granted, and for that reason did not constitute knowledge.

My concern here is not with the causal theory of knowledge in general but with the way in which one might employ the basic idea behind a causal theory of knowledge in a causal account of noninferential justification. The causal chains that lead to a person's belief might or might not involve prior beliefs. When they involve no prior beliefs – when the causal stimulus is something other than a belief, one might regard the "output" belief as noninferentially known. Foundational knowledge might be viewed as a special sort of belief caused "directly" by the fact that makes true the belief – where what makes the connection "direct" is the fact that there are no intermediate links in the causal chain involving other beliefs. Armstrong (1973) suggests that basic knowledge might be thought of as belief that registers facts about one's immediate environment in the way a thermometer registers the temperature.

Nozick's tracking account of knowledge

As we noted briefly in chapter 2, in a strikingly original account of knowledge designed to accommodate both common sense and the lure of skepticism, Robert Nozick (1981) suggests an account of knowledge closely related to the causal theory. As you will recall, on Nozick's view a belief that P constitutes knowledge when the belief "tracks" P's truth through possible worlds. As a first approximation, one might say that S's belief that P tracks the fact that P when S would believe that P if P were true, and would not believe that P if P were false. Nozick, like many other philosophers, tries to shed light on the truth conditions for the subjunctive conditionals ("if . . . then" statements that take the subjunctive mood) by invoking the metaphor of "possible worlds." S would believe P were P true if in all of the "close possible worlds" in which P is true S believes P. S wouldn't believe P were P false if S doesn't believe P in all of the "close" possible worlds in which P is false. In a world in which P is true, one finds the "close" not-P worlds by imagining a world in which not-P is the case, making as few changes as one needs to make to the actual world. So consider my true belief that there are two people in this room right now. The close possible worlds in which this is false are worlds in which one or both of the people left the room. They are not, presumably, worlds in which no one but me is a real person – the other apparent people are all automata. Nozick wisely concedes that the metaphor of possible worlds is just that – a metaphor. An informative analysis of conditionals of the form, if *P* were the case *Q* would be the case, would take us too far afield.[1] But we can still think about Nozick's analysis of knowledge employing an intuitive understanding of these conditionals.

It is the fact that we must consider counterfactuals in evaluating knowledge claims that allows us, Nozick argues, to accommodate both common sense and the force of skeptical arguments. Early in his *Meditations*, Descartes famously wondered how we could know that we aren't sound asleep having a vivid dream. Such Cartesian thought experiments inspired Hollywood to make films like *Total Recall* and *The Matrix*, films in which characters undergo hallucinatory experience so vivid as to be indistinguishable from veridical experience. Given that the evidence available to us seems quite consistent with both the view of common sense and bizarre skeptical scenarios, how can we know that we are not in the skeptical scenario? Nozick's answer is that we can't. While we do believe that we are not in the *Matrix* world, our belief couldn't possibly track that fact, since we would presumably have precisely the same belief even if we *were* in the *Matrix* world. The closest possible worlds in which we are the victims of massive hallucination are worlds in which we wouldn't believe that we were the victims of massive hallucination. On the other hand, this concession doesn't threaten the possibility of everyday knowledge. We can still know that there are people in the room because the closest worlds in which there are not (worlds in which the people left the room) might be worlds in which we would *not* believe that there are people in the room. As we saw in chapter 2, on Nozick's account of knowledge, it follows straightforwardly that knowledge isn't closed under known implication. Strangely enough, I can know that there are people in the room with me even when I don't know that I am not suffering massive hallucinatory experience causing me to believe falsely that there are people in the room.

The crude account of tracking given above doesn't quite work to Nozick's satisfaction in an account of knowledge. Nozick is aware that one can construct counterexamples in which someone would continue to believe *P* were *P* false but wouldn't believe it *in the same way*. So, to use one of Nozick's examples, suppose John's mother believes that her son arriving home from active military duty is alive and well. She believes this because he opens her door and gives her a big hug. Her neighbors, however, knowing that John's mother has a bad heart and wouldn't survive devastating news of injury to her son, had conspired to devise a complicated story that would lead her to believe that her son was alive and well even if he had died, a story that, happily, they did not need to tell. Intuitively, the conspiracy lurking in the wings is not enough to deprive the mother of knowledge based on her first-hand experience with her son. The solution, Nozick suggests, involves bringing into the account the *method* by which a belief is formed. S knows that P via a method M, when S has a true belief that P via M, would believe P in all of the close worlds in which P is true, and wouldn't believe P via M were P false. In the example just given, the mother would have believed in her son's health even if he were dead, but she wouldn't have believed it *on the basis of first-hand perception*. The account gets modified still further to take account of situations in which a belief is overdetermined. When more than one method of belief is used, we have to determine, Nozick argues, which belief-forming method is "dominant" – which would outweigh the other were they to give conflicting results. It is the belief formed by the dominant method that would need to "track" the relevant truth-maker for the belief if the belief is to constitute knowledge.

The "tracking" account of knowledge *might* be closely related to a causal account of knowledge because on some views causation itself is analyzed "counterfactually" – is analyzed employing "subjunctive" conditionals ("if . . . then . . ." statements employing the subjunctive mood). X is the immediate cause of Y, one might suggest, when Y would occur immediately following the occurrence of X, and wouldn't have occurred but for the occurrence of X. The counterfactual analysis of causation is fraught with difficulties, some of which we discussed in chapter 2, but for our present purposes we need only note that Nozick's tracking account of knowledge suggests yet another way of characterizing noninferential knowledge. We could say that a belief that P noninferentially tracks the fact that P if the belief that P tracks the fact that P in a way that (via a method that) does not involve the having of other justified beliefs. So, for example, my belief that I'm in pain might track the fact that I am in pain. In the close worlds in which I'm in pain I believe that I am, and in the close worlds in which I'm not in pain, I don't believe that I'm in pain. Furthermore, the causal mechanism by which the belief tracks the pain (whatever it is) doesn't seem to involve any intermediate beliefs. By contrast, when I read in a newspaper that the leader of a country has been assassinated, I do form the belief that the event occurred, but, arguably, only as a result of certain relatively stable background beliefs concerning such truths as the reliability of newspapers like this. The tracking mechanism involves intermediate and background beliefs.

Goldman's reliabilism

Not long after advancing the causal theory of knowing Goldman returned to a justified true belief account of knowledge, but with a radically different, externalist, account of justification (developed in Goldman 1979, 1986, and 1988). Again, beginning with a rough characterization, the idea is that a belief is justified when it results from a reliable belief-forming process. If I'm so constituted that I believe that I did X whenever I seem to remember having done X, and beliefs formed this way are usually true, then this way of forming beliefs is reliable and the resulting beliefs are justified. In contrast to internal state internalism, the idea is that the *history* of a belief – the way in which the belief was formed – is critical to its epistemic status. What made Goldman's view so attractive to both Goldman and his followers is that it seemed to accommodate the plausible idea that when a belief is justified it has a virtue. There is something good about justified beliefs. From the epistemic perspective, virtue has to do with truth. Because we want to allow for the possibility of a justified/rational belief that is false, we can't simply identify justified belief with true belief, but we can acknowledge an intimate connection between justification and truth by understanding the beliefs that are justified as those that come about in a way that usually results in the having of true beliefs. For reasons that are obvious, the reliability of the "belief-forming" mechanism can't be defined in terms of the actual frequency with which true beliefs are produced. There might be some way of forming beliefs that is employed only once resulting in a true belief. For example, I might be the only person who ever attempts to predict the outcome of an election by putting the names of the candidates in a hat and picking one of the names. I only do this once and by chance pick the winner. We hardly want to allow that the way in which the belief is formed is 100 percent reliable because it resulted in all (one!) true beliefs – no false beliefs. One obvious solution is to turn once again to counterfactuals. The reliable belief-forming processes are those that *would* usually result in true belief *were* the belief-forming mechanism used to generate a great many beliefs. Because we are convinced that the "names in a hat" way of predicting elections would not in the long run result in true predictions we are convinced that this way of forming beliefs is unreliable.

The move to counterfactuals may not by itself eliminate the problem. Plantinga (1993) introduces the term "warrant" to replace the term "justification" in identifying the feature of belief that he thinks should be of most interest to the epistemologist. He suggests that we define warrant as whatever it is that when added to true belief yields knowledge. He objects to thinking of justification as the "third" condition for knowledge primarily because he believes there is that normative dimension to justification that we discussed and rejected in chapter 3.[2] In any event, he thinks that one can imagine a belief-forming process that satisfies the counterfactual test for reliability even though it clearly would not bestow on the resulting belief warrant (or as I might prefer to put it, justification of a sort relevant to knowledge). To illustrate his concern, imagine that most of us are superstitious and believe that breaking a mirror portends a long period of bad luck. As it turns out, there is a very powerful immortal being who finds somewhat comical this belief of ours and who decides to punish us for having such odd beliefs by bringing about bad luck for all of us (now and in the future) who come to believe that we will have bad luck based on such bad evidence. In this situation, the belief-forming mechanism satisfies the counterfactual test for reliability – it not only results in mostly true beliefs, but it would continue to result in such beliefs were we to employ the method for an indefinitely long period of time. Yet the beliefs in question surely do not acquire warrant or justification. Plantinga's own view is that we need to introduce the notion of a cognitive faculty *designed* in such a way that it allows us to get at the truth most of the time when it operates in a situation for which it was designed. Warranted beliefs are those that result from the employment of such a faculty, a faculty that is functioning properly. Plantinga invites us to understand the critical concept of design, at least initially, in any way that is intuitively plausible. Some sympathetic to his general idea might appeal to the evolution of the cognitive faculty in order to explain this talk of design. A belief-forming mechanism is designed to produce a certain kind of belief in a certain kind of environment if that way of forming belief has been "selected" through evolution. Plantinga himself doesn't see why nature would select for true beliefs (he thinks one can easily imagine a world in which the right combination of desires and false beliefs do quite nicely in ensuring survival) and suggests that we should instead identify the design of a belief-forming process in terms of the purpose for which it was created by a conscious designer – God. However we understand design, though, we have another way of trying to understand the critical reliability in terms of which we are trying to develop a concept of reliability for use in an account of justification (warrant).[3]

Our initial characterization of reliabilism is far too crude. It fails to capture the foundationalist structure of a reliabilist account of justification. Like traditional foundationalists, Goldman's account of justification is explicitly recursive. There are two kinds of belief-forming processes. One is a belief-dependent, conditionally reliable process. The other is a belief-independent, unconditionally reliable process. A belief-dependent, conditionally reliable process takes as its input at least some beliefs states and produces other beliefs. The process is conditionally reliable insofar as the "output" beliefs are usually true when the input beliefs are true.[4] So if I'm a rational human being and believe that P and that if P then Q, that might result in my believing Q. The process is a paradigm of a conditionally reliable process that is 100 percent reliable. When the "input" beliefs are true, the "output" beliefs are true 100 percent of the time.

Shall we say that a belief is justified when it results from a conditionally reliable belief-forming process? Of course not. The "input" beliefs might be wildly irrational even if the process is conditionally reliable. In the example given above, I might have believed P and if P then Q with no reason whatsoever. Again, garbage in – garbage out! Conditionally reliable belief-forming processes generate justified beliefs only if the input beliefs are *justified*. But now, in characterizing the way in which belief-dependent conditionally reliable processes yield justified beliefs, we invoked the very concept of justified belief we are trying to illuminate. The solution, of course, is to find a kind of justification that doesn't derive in whole or in part from the having of other justified belief. We need a *base* clause for our recursive definition of justification (see chapter 3). Goldman finds the base clause in a belief-independent unconditionally reliable belief-forming process. He says that a belief-forming process is belief-independent and unconditionally reliable when it takes as its input something other than belief and when its output beliefs are usually true (or would be true most of the time were the belief-forming process extensively employed). So let's take as our example, once again, belief about pain. When I'm in pain I believe that I am. Human beings, Goldman might argue, are hard wired so as to "monitor" some of their internal states. My pain causes me to believe that I'm in pain and the causal process does not seem to involve any intermediate beliefs. It's a process that is close to 100 percent reliable.[5]

Notice that on this characterization of noninferential justification, such justification might "guarantee" the truth of what is believed even if the believer who possesses that justification might find it perfectly conceivable that the belief in question is false. As we'll see, this might turn into a source of dissatisfaction with the view. It is also important to realize, however, that the reliabilist is in a position to divorce noninferential justification entirely from infallible justification. For a belief to be noninferentially justified it is enough that its "input" are stimuli other than belief-states, and the output belief results from an unconditionally reliable process. Reliability comes in degrees. It is perfectly open to the reliabilist to count a process as reliable if its output beliefs are true 51 percent of the time. The justification that results will, of course, be correspondingly weak. It turns out, then, that on a reliabilist account of noninferential justification, noninferential justification need not be any stronger, or any better, than inferential justification. Contra Descartes, the reliabilist can reject completely the idea that foundations for justification need have some particularly secure epistemic standing.

With the concept of noninferentially justified belief we are positioned to offer a recursive analysis of justified belief: A belief is justified when either (1) it is produced by a belief-independent,[6] unconditionally reliable process or (2) it is produced by a belief-dependent, conditionally reliable process whose input beliefs are justified. Although (2) invokes the concept of justified belief it does so harmlessly because we understand the recursive structure of our definition. More intuitively, we can say that a belief is justified when either it is produced by a belief-independent unconditionally reliable process *or* it is produced by a conditionally reliable belief-dependent process whose input beliefs were produced by a belief-independent unconditionally reliable process, *or* it is produced by a conditionally reliable belief-dependent process whose input beliefs were produced by a belief-dependent conditionally reliable belief-forming process whose input beliefs were produced by a belief-independent unconditionally reliable process *or* . . . Like all foundationalists, the reliabilist insists that all justified beliefs inherit their justification ultimately from their noninferentially justified "ancestors."

Criticisms of externalism

I have tried to highlight some of the main features of three versions of externalist foundationalism – a causal theory, a tracking analysis, and reliabilism. While these aren't the only versions of externalism (we saw earlier that the coherence theory has its externalist version), the three I summarized are certainly among the most influential. Each view has encountered many criticisms. Some of those criticisms are directed at the account of inferential justification the view offers, an account we'll examine more carefully in the next chapter. But we can profitably examine criticisms of the views' accounts of noninferential (foundational) justification/ knowledge.

We can broadly distinguish two sorts of criticisms. One focuses on the details of the externalist's specific account of noninferential justification, where often the critic is receptive to the suggestion that appropriate modification of the view might deal with the alleged problem. The other sort of criticism is more general and fundamental. This critic purports to have found an objection that strikes at the very heart of any externalist account of justification.

Detailed Objections

The causal theory

Causal theories of any concept have a terrible time dealing with so-called "deviant" causal chains. So, for example, many philosophers suggest that visual perception should be understood in terms of a causal relation between the object perceived and some internal visual experience had by the perceiver. On a crude version of the view, S sees X when X causes in S a visual experience. But causal connections can be convoluted in a way that presents problems for naïve causal theories. A mad but brilliant scientist might have stolen my brain in the middle of the night. That brain is now sitting in a vat while the mad scientist stimulates it so as to produce massive hallucinatory experience. Rather than conjure up the "plot" of the hallucinatory experience from scratch, however, the scientist looks out his window and produces those brain states, among others, that produce a visual experience just like the one he is having of the cars parked outside. In a roundabout way the cars are figuring in a causal chain that results in my "envatted" brain having a visual experience, but it is doubtful that we want to allow that I am actually (veridically) seeing those cars. As we saw earlier, the possibility of similar deviant chains leading from the truth maker of a belief to the belief spell trouble for naïve causal theories of knowing.

Goldman, as we saw, tried to deal with the problem by adding the requirement that the causal chain leading from truth-maker to belief be roughly along the lines envisioned by the believer. When it comes to non-inferentially justified belief, however, the initial problem with that suggestion seems to be the implausibility of supposing that the believer has any view of how the belief in question came about. Frankly, I haven't got a clue as to what the physiological story is that hooks up my pain with the resulting belief that I'm in pain. I suppose I do think of it as more or less direct, but I also probably know enough about the body to realize that even relatively direct causal chains have indefinitely many links (think about how many links there are in the causal chain that leads from damage to my toe to the brain state that produces pain).

But even if one can make plausible the suggestion that direct knowledge involves causal chains that match the background beliefs of the believer, we are faced with the fact that there might be such a causal chain that is exactly of the sort envisioned by the believer despite the fact that the believer's view is epistemically crazy! It's hard to say which belief-forming causal chains are noninferential and which are not (which involve intermediate beliefs and which don't). On this sort of view, that question is to be answered by empirical research. Inspired by a view of Plantinga's (2000), let's suppose that my belief that there is a God is in fact caused by the fact that God himself instructed the Holy Spirit to whisper in my ear in the middle of the night that God exists, an act that in fact successfully induces in me the belief that God exists. Would I know that God exists? Probably not, Goldman might argue, for the odd causal chain leading to the belief wasn't envisioned by me. But suppose, out of the blue, I came up with precisely this hypothesis as to how I ended up believing in God. It just seemed to me a plausible explanation of how I arrived at the belief. Would anyone really suppose that my belief that God exists is a good example of foundational knowledge? At the very least, we would surely demand of the believer that he had good reason to suppose that this is the correct causal explanation of his belief. But, of course, if the believer had such a justified belief, it would be the possession of such justification that is securing epistemic rationality for the belief that God exists.

Nozick's tracking account

As we noted in chapter 2, Nozick brazenly suggests that the fact that his account of knowledge forces one to reject closure principles is a virtue of the account. There is an old joke in philosophy that one philosopher's modus ponens is another's modus tollens. From the premise that Nozick's account of knowledge is correct and the truth that if that account is correct then closure principles are false, we can infer that closure principles are false (modus ponens). But it is surely at least as plausible to argue that closure principles are about as obvious as any principle offered by an epistemologist, and if Nozick's account of knowledge requires rejecting closure principles, so much the worse for Nozick's account of knowledge (modus tollens). If I *really* am in no position to know that I'm not living in a *Matrix* world, then by God I really don't know that I'm sitting in a chair in front of a computer right now![7]

Furthermore, given the similarities between a causal theory and a tracking account of knowledge, it is not surprising that objections to the former will often be objections to the latter. If a belief that is caused in a wild way by the truth-maker for the belief is not epistemically justified, then a belief that tracks the truth of the proposition believed, but does so in a "wild" way, will not constitute knowledge either.

Reliabilism

Goldman himself worried about a number of objections to the reliabilist account of justification in general and noninferential justification in particular. Again, it is not clear which beliefs are supposed to be generated by belief-independent processes. In my discussion of Gettier problems in chapter 2 I suggested that there may often be a vast array of background beliefs playing a role in justifying, and perhaps even causing, ordinary everyday beliefs. To be sure, when I conclude that there is a bus bearing down on me, I don't run through some conscious inference from the character of my visual experience, the environment in which I find myself, and the likelihood that all this indicates a rather large and potentially dangerous vehicle moving rapidly towards me. If I had to laboriously run through such inferences before reaching conclusions about the world around me I would have long since perished. But it is still not clear that the vast network of dispositional beliefs "stored" in my memory are not causally active in producing the "spontaneous" conclusion I reach. Again, for the reliabilist, as for the causal theorist and the tracking theorist, it is an empirical question as to which beliefs, if any, are noninferentially known or justified.

Let's suppose, rather implausibly I would argue, that simple perceptual beliefs about objects immediately before one and perhaps beliefs about not-so-distant past events based on memory are both examples of beliefs produced by belief-independent, unconditionally reliable processes. Does the fact that they are so produced make them epistemically justified? In his earliest attempt to develop reliabilism (1979), Goldman himself considered the example of the person who has beliefs about the past but who is the victim of a rather elaborate conspiracy. His doctors, loved ones, and friends have agreed to convince him that he is suffering massive hallucination with respect to the past. He has a rare disease, they tell him, that results in the brain manufacturing "false" memories. It is a conspiracy, however. There is nothing wrong with his rather excellent memory. Everything he seems to remember having done he actually did, and despite now having excellent reason not to trust his memory he can't help believe what his memory dictates. His beliefs about the past, that is, are in fact produced by a highly reliable memory mechanism. While the hard-core reliabilist could, of course, bite the bullet and argue that in such a situation the person in question had a perfectly justified belief about the past, Goldman was unwilling to bite that bullet. It seemed to him that the availability of rather strong evidence indicating that he shouldn't trust his memory was enough to defeat whatever justification he might otherwise have had.

To deal with the problem Goldman suggested a revision to the base clause in his recursive analysis of justification:

> If S's belief in p at [time] t results from a reliable cognitive process, and there is no reliable or conditionally reliable process available to S which, had it been used by S in addition to the process actually used, would have resulted in S's not believing p at t, then S's belief in p at t is justified. (Goldman, 1979, p. 20)

The revision might seem initially plausible but it faces a number of instructive problems. First, one might wonder just how to cash out the notion of an unused but available belief-forming process. In what sense is it true that the victim of conspiracy had available to him an alternative method of forming beliefs which he could have used in addition to the ones he did use? By hypothesis, he obviously *didn't* get himself to trust the authority figures who were assuring him that his memory was not to be trusted. If the influence of vivid memory was so strong that he *couldn't* but believe what it indicated, does that influence our judgment about whether his belief was epistemically justified?

Of course, what we really want to say, but had better not say, is that there was *evidence* S had which S *should* have used in addition to the data of memory. There was justification for S to believe that his memory was unreliable and that should have been taken into account by him in reaching appropriate conclusions about the past. But a base clause in a recursive analysis of justification should not invoke the concept of justification. We are trying to find a non-circular way of characterizing a condition sufficient for noninferential justification that we can then employ in a characterization of inferential justification. The difficulty facing Goldman's revision can be put more formally this way. We start with the idea that being produced by a belief-independent, unconditionally reliable process is sufficient for justification. We then get cold feet because we realize that a person whose belief is produced in this way might have good epistemic reason to believe that the belief in question is not produced reliably. We then want to suggest that a belief is justified when it is produced by a belief-independent process provided that there are no other unconditionally *or conditionally* reliable belief-forming processes available which would yield different results when used in conjunction with the belief-independent process. But if we think back to the relevance of conditionally reliable belief-forming processes to epistemic justification we remember that the availability of a conditionally reliable belief-forming process would only be epistemically relevant to a subject's epistemic justification if the subject had justified beliefs to serve as input to the process. But then the more perspicuous representation of the new proposed base clause is this:

> If S's belief in p at time t results from a belief-independent unconditionally reliable process, and there is no belief-independent, unconditionally reliable process which, had it been used by S, would have resulted in his not believing p, and there is no belief-dependent process which is conditionally reliable that could have been used by S to process certain *justified* beliefs so as to result in him not believing p at t, then S's belief in p at t is justified.

Again, one sees clearly the problem. In invoking the concept of epistemic justification one renders the account circular.

There might be a general lesson to be learned here for all foundationalists. In our survey of traditional foundationalisms we saw that the traditional foundationalist wanted to secure a very tight connection between noninferential justification and truth – so tight that no additional evidence could defeat noninferential justification. If one allows that the conditions that generate noninferential justification might still allow the noninferentially justified belief to be false – indeed that noninferentially justified beliefs might not enjoy very strong justification – then it is going to be very hard to suppose that one couldn't couple the presence of those conditions with competing counter-evidence that destroys the justification. That concession, however, is tantamount to allowing that we haven't really isolated a condition that is sufficient for (noninferential) justification. We need such a condition, however, if we are committed to a recursive analysis of justification.

There may be solutions available to the reliabilist, and for that matter to other foundationalists who seek to allow weak noninferential justification. One is to abandon the idea of a recursive analysis of justification. The reliabilist could still introduce the concept of prima facie noninferential justification understood in terms of possessing non-doxastic data (states that are not belief states) that could be processed by an unconditionally reliable processes. But one could define the epistemic status of S's belief that P at time t in terms of whether *all* of the data available to one at time t processed by *all* of the belief-independent processes available whose output beliefs were in turn processed by all of the belief-dependent processes available would yield the belief that P, where the reliability that determines the epistemic status of the belief that P is the reliability of the "giant" process made up of all of these sub processes acting together.

In adopting the above revision of reliabilism, we will also solve another problem that obviously faces the view. On crude statements of reliabilism a belief that P which is the end product of a series of belief-producing processes, each of which is reliable in the relevant way, will be justified. But if the processes are not 100 percent reliable and are independent of one another, one "loses" probability through the additional layering of active belief-producing processes. There might be a 90 percent chance of getting through the first processing without error, a 90 percent chance of getting through the second without error, and so on for twenty or thirty processes. But the chance of getting through them all might be exceedingly small. (Think again about making free throws in basketball. Very good free throw shooters have a high probability of making each free throw they attempt, but the chance that they'll make thirty in a row is remote.) By insisting that the reliability that dictates the justificatory status of a belief is the reliability of the giant complex process which is the simultaneous operation of all processes on all available data and output beliefs, we take care of the loss of probability through the accumulative use of belief-producing processes.

There is another technical problem facing all versions of reliabilism – *the generality problem*. So far we have been throwing around talk of belief-forming processes and their conditional or unconditional reliability as though we had some relatively clear idea of how to individuate belief-forming processes and their inputs and outputs. We are going to need to figure out what *kind* of process is responsible for a given belief if we are to be even in a position to understand talk about its reliability – a concept that requires us to make sense of that *same* (kind of) process generating indefinitely many beliefs. Individuating belief-forming processes is no easy matter, however.

The first task one must complete in individuating a process is to figure out what precisely we are regarding as the input to the process. When push comes to shove, a belief-forming process is probably best understood as links in a causal chain – probably a sequence of causes and effects that take place in the brain and eventually results in a belief. But what shall we take to be the critical "first" links in the causal chain? How far back should we go? Let's make the question clear with an example. Consider a perceptually formed belief. I think there is a tree outside my window. The belief didn't just "pop" into existence – it had a cause. What was the cause? Well we could say that the input processed by the brain was a visual sensation. Philosophers argue a great deal with each other about the status of sensation, but for now let's understand it as something that *results* from light hitting the retina of the eye. Of course we could take the input to be the change in the retina. Or for that matter, we could describe the entire process as light bounding off the surface of a tree and hitting the retina producing a visual experience which then gets "interpreted" as a tree.[8] Which description of the process we offer affects dramatically the reliability of the process. The last process is 100 percent reliable. Whenever light reflects off of a tree and initiates a causal chain that results in my believing that there is a tree there, the output belief is true. But surely that's too easy – that's a sophistical way to generate the kind of reliability that would intuitively give one justification.

Goldman, and most other reliabilists, suggest that what we are most interested in is the believer and his reliability as a truth seeker as he moves from context to context. For that reason, we don't want to include too much of a description of the environment in our characterization of the input to a belief-forming process. We would do better to identify the "data" that gets processed as that which results from the impingement on the body by outside forces. But if we make such a move we face more difficult questions. Consider memory. I seem to remember putting my car keys by the kitchen sink and that produces the belief that that's where they are. Is the process reliable? Well, what is the process? It's the familiar causal chain that proceeds from seeming to remember and results in belief. But are we lumping together those situations in which I seem to remember relatively recent experiences, with situations in which I seem to remember distant events? Are we taking the apparent memories of very old and stubbornly optimistic people and the beliefs those memories generate, with the memories of young people? It makes a huge difference. I'm getting to that nasty stage where the fact that I seem to remember having done something with my car keys isn't correlated all that well with the present location of the keys. Suppose a strange disease wipes out 99 percent of people with good memories. You are one of the fortunate few whose memory is still reliable. Do you really want the fact that you are surrounded by people who constantly get confused about the past based on their frequent misleading memory "experiences" to affect your ability to have perfectly justified beliefs about the past?

Just as the same memory process can occur in people with good memories and people with bad memories (where the critical difference between the two sorts of people probably has more to do with what causes the apparent memory), so also the same belief-forming process might be reliable in one environment and be unreliable in another. Suppose I'm an astronaut who crash lands on a distant planet where odd features of the atmosphere distort radically the colors objects appear to have – objects that are really red, for example, appear blue. I live the rest of my life on the planet never catching on and, as a result, building up impressive numbers of false beliefs about the colors of the objects around me. Is my belief-forming process the same one that used to operate rather effectively in getting me true beliefs on Earth? Suppose that, over time, generations of space travelers begin to inhabit this planet until finally the belief forming process "seem to see red – believe that it is red" generates more false beliefs than true beliefs. What shall we say about the reliability of the process and the epistemic justification of beliefs about colors? Do the remaining inhabitants of Earth still have justified beliefs because their color-belief-forming processes are not the same as the inhabitants of the color-distorted world? Did they have justified beliefs for awhile until the false beliefs finally start to outnumber the true beliefs? Perhaps, as Sosa (1991) suggests, we should relativize epistemic justification (and the reliability that is crucial to it) to an environment. Perhaps we should say that the very same process can be reliable at one time in one environment, but not at another time or in another environment. But still, how fine-grained should our description of the environment be relative to which we try to understand the relativized conception of reliability?[9]

The above problem is not unrelated to one we considered in introducing Plantinga's conception of a warranted belief as belief that is produced by a cognitive capacity that is functioning properly in the environment for which it was designed. Again, one might think of that environment as one envisioned by a designer, or one might think of it as the environment that played a critical role during the evolutionary process that selected for that way of forming beliefs. About the example given above, Plantinga would claim, presumably, that once I leave the planet for which my sensory apparatus was designed, the beliefs formed lose their warrant. But if we are interested in getting at a concept of justification, or rationality, or even warrant, when warrant is understood as a positive epistemic property and is understood in such a way that there can be warranted false beliefs, it is not clear that we are getting the right result by refusing to recognize that my beliefs retain warrant when I move to the "distorting" environment. As long as there is no reason to believe that the environment is critically different, why wouldn't it be perfectly reasonable to believe what I do about the colors of the objects around me? But this brings us to more fundamental objections to not just reliabilism in particular, but to externalism in general.

Fundamental Objections

Hallucination and justification

Internalists think that the externalist's approach to understanding epistemic concepts is fundamentally and hopelessly flawed. I'll try to illustrate the nature of the internalist's dissatisfaction with externalism focusing on reliabilism, but with the understanding that similar concerns are supposed to afflict other versions of externalism. The basic idea is that a belief's causal origin, its ability to track facts, or its reliable source is neither necessary nor sufficient for its epistemic status. Consider first a counterexample that bothered Goldman himself. It seems that we can imagine two people who have precisely the same experiential evidence upon which to rely, one of whom lives in the world we take this to be, and the other of whom lives in a *Matrix* world (or a world in which mad scientists are stimulating brains in a vat, or there is an evil demon playing a massive prank on conscious beings by telepathically producing massive hallucinatory experience). To be sure, we might not have any problem reaching the conclusion that one of these individuals knows truths about his physical environment while the other does not. As long as there is a truth condition for knowledge that is not tied to justification, virtually every philosopher is going to be an externalist about *knowledge*.[10] But there surely does seem to be something very odd about the suggestion that one of our individuals has justified beliefs about his physical environment, while the other does not. Surely, whatever is reasonable for you to believe about the physical objects before you, is equally reasonable for your *Matrix*-world double to believe. The victim of *Matrix*-world deception would be crazy not to believe what you believe. You yourself would have precisely the same beliefs were you to be suddenly transported (without your knowledge) to the world of massive hallucination.

Again, because we are focusing on noninferential justification in this chapter, let us suppose (implausibly, as I suggested earlier) that perception is a belief-independent process. While the two individuals described above have qualitatively indistinguishable sense experience (and we may also suppose apparent memories), one of them, by hypothesis, is generating countless true beliefs about his physical environment, while the other is generating countless false beliefs about his environment. The veridical perceiver has beliefs produced by an unconditionally reliable process; the victim of massive hallucination has beliefs produced by an unconditionally unreliable process. According to the reliabilist, the one should have justified, rational beliefs, while the other has unjustified, irrational beliefs. But we have this overpowering inclination to think that this is just wrong. We are convinced that however reasonable it is for the one to believe what he believes, it is just that reasonable for the other to have similar beliefs. Bad luck might deprive the one of knowledge, but it surely can't deprive him of justified belief.

Unfortunately, the critic who takes this line of attack often combines it with remarks about the normativity of justification. You will recall that in chapter 3 we discussed the question of how, if at all, epistemic concepts are properly regarded as normative concepts, and reached the conclusion that claims about the normativity of the epistemic were highly problematic. As we saw, one way of trying to tie epistemic judgments to normative judgments involves claiming that there is a tie between epistemic evaluation of a belief and a kind of praise or blame of either the belief or the believer. If someone's belief is justified it is OK for the person to have the belief. The believer is (epistemically) blameless for having the belief. We won't criticize the person for having the belief. If we decide that a person's belief is unjustified, we are criticizing either the belief or the believer. We think that the person is to be faulted for having the belief. We think that the belief is one that the person shouldn't have.

If one endorsed these sorts of connections between epistemic evaluation and criticism, praise and blame, and judgments about what people should or shouldn't believe, one can immediately see how they would be deployed in support of the attack against reliabilism. The victim of massive hallucination is hardly to be *blamed* for believing what he believes. How could we in good conscience *criticize* someone for believing what we know *we* would believe were we in the same epistemic predicament?

But normativity is a double-edged sword. In response, the reliabilist can make the distinction made in chapter 3 between the evaluation of a subject and the evaluation of a belief. From the fact that a believer is not to be blamed or criticized for a belief, it doesn't follow that there is nothing defective about the belief. But when we shift our attention to the hallucination-induced belief, what is supposed to be defective about it? Well, it is after all false, and other things being equal, isn't it better to have true beliefs than false beliefs? Furthermore, it was produced by a process which, by hypothesis, generated countless false beliefs, and other

93

things being equal, isn't it better to be the kind of believer whose beliefs are produced by mechanisms that get you at the truth more often than not? Isn't the "raison d'être" of belief to get at the truth, and can't the reliabilist point to the obvious fact that if you can't have true belief then at least you can have belief that originates in such a way as to give you a good chance at getting at the truth?

The above response to the argument from hallucination against reliabilism tries to co-opt arguments that rest on the alleged normativity of epistemic concepts. The reliabilist tries to show how on perfectly ordinary understandings of good and bad belief, and good and bad ways of forming belief, reliabilism can make as good a case as any other view that it captures a significant sort of virtue that beliefs and ways of forming beliefs might display. But the best counter to all of this is to let the dust surrounding normativity settle, and point out again that we simply find it very difficult to regard the victim of massive hallucination as having formed epistemically irrational beliefs about his environment. He is no more irrational than is the jury who convicts a defendant based on evidence that was cleverly trumped up by the prosecutor. Rational juries go where the evidence takes them. And rational believers cleverly deceived by sensation, go where the evidence takes them.

As I indicated above, Goldman himself worried a great deal about the above objection, raising it himself in his earliest (1979) attempt to develop a reliabilist account of justification. In a subsequent book (1986), he tried to disarm the objection by relativizing the critical definition of reliability for a belief-forming process to "normal" worlds. Roughly, normal worlds are those worlds that are in certain *fundamental* respects just like the world we *take* this to be. The idea wasn't a happy one. It wasn't easy to figure out what the fundamental respects were supposed to be (though it was clear any world envisioned by a radical skepticism wasn't going to count as "normal"). Worse, though, whatever attraction reliabilism might have had to those who wanted a "tight" connection between having epistemically justified beliefs and having beliefs that are mostly true is now completely lost. The actual world might not be a normal world, and our "epistemically justified beliefs" might be produced by processes that are in fact pathetically unreliable.

To his credit, Goldman dropped the normal worlds approach to dealing with the objection and eventually settled on a dramatically bifurcated account of epistemic justification (1988). He distinguished strong and weak justification. Strong justification is captured by a hard-core reliabilism. Weak justification has more to do with forming beliefs in ways that conform to community standards, where the believer in question has bought into those standards. We can then say of our inhabitant of the *Matrix* world that his beliefs were weakly justified but strongly unjustified. This reli-abilist tries to assuage the critic by giving the beliefs of the victim of hallucination some sort of positive epistemic status, while insisting that in another clear sense, when you get right down to it, people who form beliefs in demon-world or *Matrix*-world environments have the kind of seriously defective beliefs it is appropriate to criticize as unjustified.

When a philosopher must resort to this sort of bifurcation, it is at least time to be suspicious. It is not that we don't often use the same term with a different meaning. There are uncontroversial examples. The bank you put your money in doesn't have much to do with the bank of the river. But it is hardly plausible to suppose that we can attribute that sort of straightforward ambiguity to the terms "epistemic justification" or "epistemic rationality." Goldman is trying to develop two senses of "epistemic justification" – concepts that are of interest to the epistemologist. There is another sort of ambiguity that one often does encounter. The meaning of "courageous" when it is used to characterize a country is not, I would argue, the same as the meaning of "courageous" when it is used to characterize a person. But it is not hard to see what the connection between the two uses might be. The courage of a country can be defined in terms of some group of people who make up the country (its people, its leaders, or its military, for example). But Goldman's two concepts of justification don't seem to have this sort of relation to one another either. Neither concept is somehow parasitic upon the other. In fact, it is hard to escape the conclusion that the concept of weak justification is introduced for the sole purpose of acknowledging the strength of the internalist's criticism of reliabilism.

We discussed this objection in connection with the reliabilist's version of externalism. It should be obvious, however, that if the internalist has successfully identified a weakness with reliabilism, a similar problem would face both causal theories and tracking accounts of noninferential justification and knowledge. Our two individuals with seemingly identical subjective justification might have their respective beliefs caused in quite different ways. One individual might inhabit a world in which the belief tracks the relevant truth-maker for the belief while the other lives in a world in which the belief fails to track the relevant truth-maker. In neither case would we want to claim that the person has either knowledge or a justified belief. The objection to reliabilism can easily enough be extended to other paradigm externalist accounts of noninferential justification.

BonJour's objections

The first objection to externalism (illustrated primarily in connection with reliabilism) called into question the necessity of the externalist's proposed conditions for justification. It seemed plausible that one could have powerful justification even if the resulting belief was not reliably produced, or caused in the way required by the causal theorist. BonJour (1985) also calls into question the sufficiency of the conditions the externalist proposes. In short, he thinks he can imagine situations in which the conditions proposed by the externalist as an analysis of justification are satisfied even though, intuitively, the person who satisfies those conditions does not have a justified belief. Again, let us look at the argument as it might be directed at the reliabilist, keeping in mind that it could be suitably modified to attack other paradigm externalist analyses of justification.

BonJour starts with an example that even most reliabilists find compelling – one rather similar to the hypothetical situation Goldman himself first raised in arguing that an earlier formulation of reliabilism required revision. BonJour asks us to consider someone who in fact has clairvoyant powers. Our hypothetical person occasionally believes on the basis of "premonitions" that some disaster has or will occur, and is always right. Let us also suppose, however, that the person has no independent reason to suppose that the beliefs based on premonitions are true. The person has no access to newspapers, or other public sources of information that would allow him to independently establish that his absolute conviction that a major earthquake took place was in fact correct. Indeed, let us further suppose that our hypothetical person with this uncanny ability to predict disaster has an enormous body of evidence indicating that there is no such thing as premonition. Despite possessing the power, he surely is irrational to believe what he believes. As we discussed earlier, Goldman himself recognizes the problem. When a person with perfectly veridical memory had powerful epistemic reason to believe that his memory is unreliable, that person's beliefs about the past resulting from memory are intuitively irrational. The person should have at the very least withheld belief.

BonJour then asks an important rhetorical question. Suppose that instead of having positive evidence indicating that there is no such thing as clairvoyance, our hypothetical person simply lacks evidence one way or the other. Would this really render rational those beliefs based on a power that the person has no reason to believe exists? The answer to the rhetorical question is supposed to be clear. Reliable processes, beliefs caused by facts that are their truth makers, beliefs that track the truth of what is

96

believed – none of these generate justification until the person has some reason to believe that the process is reliable, the belief is caused by the truth-maker, or the belief does track the truth of what is believed. Of course, if one possessed such evidence, *that* would be the source of the belief's positive epistemic status. We'll return to this topic in our discussion of the way in which internalists and externalists respond to skeptical arguments.

Epistemic justification and assurance

There is a more general worry that almost all internalists have with externalist accounts of noninferential justification. The concern is that the externalists have failed to capture a philosophically interesting concept of justification, that externalists have simply changed the subject matter of epistemology by redefining the terms of the classical debate. But all this is painfully vague. The reliabilist, for example, claims that reliabilism gives us a perfectly clear account of a virtue that a belief might possess. It is, after all, surely good if we are people who are designed so as to gain truth and avoid falsehood. We want to be able to respond to appropriate stimuli with true belief. If we can't get it right all of the time, then at least it's good that we get it right most of the time.

All this is true. And evaluating the beliefs of others, I actually suspect that the externalist may be right in suggesting that we are sometimes mainly interested in whether the subject of our evaluation is getting at the truth effectively. The internalist is convinced, however, that matters change when we adopt the first-person perspective.

I take my first philosophy class and read with interest Descartes who warns me that I have accepted much without a great deal of reflection. He also warns me that people are caused to believe all sorts of things by factors that are epistemically irrelevant. He suggests that I carefully reexamine my beliefs to ensure that they admit of no possibility of error, but we can perhaps modify his recommendation slightly. It might be a good idea to reexamine much of what we believe to ensure that those beliefs are rational. Let's suppose I believe that there is a God, roughly along the lines set out by the Judeo-Christian tradition. It doesn't require a whole lot of sophistication to realize that it is no accident that people like me, growing up in a culture dominated by the Judeo-Christian tradition, are more likely than not to have such beliefs, at least at some time or other in their development. But I'm now waxing philosophical. I'm taking Cartesian advice and I'm trying to assure myself that this isn't some odd, irrational belief.

The reliabilist tells me, or at least should tell me, that my belief in God might not only be justified, but be noninferentially justified. It was long part of many religious traditions that the "Chosen Ones" had God's existence revealed through "divine inspiration." If there is such a thing as divine inspiration, it's not a bad candidate for a belief-independent, unconditionally reliable belief-forming process. As we saw earlier, it's also not a bad candidate for a belief caused "directly" by the fact that makes it true. It's also a pretty good candidate, I imagine, for a belief that would track the truth of what is believed. So maybe I've got myself a noninferentially justified belief in God's existence, at least as the reliabilist, the causal theorist, or the tracking theorist understands noninferential justification. But should I possess such justification, would it do me any good *at all* in satisfying my intellectual curiosity? Should I possess such justification, would it do me any good *at all* in giving myself the assurance that was shaken by my brief excursion into philosophy? Internalists think that possessing the sort of justification defined by externalists would be utterly irrelevant to possessing the kind of justification we seek when we try to put our beliefs on a secure footing – the kind of justification that gives us assurance.

Now it may be that internalists want something they can't have. We'll explore this possibility in chapter 7 when we explore the way in which internalists and externalists will respond to the problem of skepticism.

Suggested readings

BonJour, Laurence and Sosa, Ernest. 2003. *Epistemic Justification*, part II. Oxford: Blackwell.

Conee, Earl and Feldman, Richard. 1998. "The Generality Problem for Reliabilism." *Philosophical Studies*, 89, 1–29.

Goldman, Alvin. 1979. "What Is Justified Belief?" in George Pappas, ed., *Justification and Knowledge*. Dordrecht: Reidel.

Notes

1   In fact, it is one of the more intractable of philosophical problems.
2   He doesn't think (nor do I) that whether a person is blameless or not for what they believe is relevant to an epistemic assessment of their belief – certainly not an epistemic assessment relevant to an attribution of knowledge.
3   I should emphasize that Plantinga does not think of his view as a version of reliabilism, but rather as an alternative to reliabilism. In treating it as the

former, I am not denying the very important differences there are between Plantinga's view and more common forms of reliabilism.

4   It might be no accident that the rise in popularity of reliabilism coincided with our becoming fully enmeshed in the computer age. Just as working (effective computers) generate appropriate outputs from input signals, so effective epistemic agents generate appropriate beliefs given relevant stimuli.

5   We might also be able to monitor in this way our own belief states. For this reason one must be careful in one's reliabilist characterization of noninferential justification. It's tempting to say that a belief is noninferentially justified when it takes as input something other than a belief. But if the having of a belief causes one to believe that one has the belief, that might be an example of an unconditionally reliable process that takes as its input a belief and results in a noninferentially justified belief. Note though that the justificatory status of the input belief is irrelevant to the justification of the output belief. For a discussion of this point see Jennifer Wilson (2004).

6   Though see the footnote immediately preceding this.

7   I discussed what I took to be a particularly embarrassing consequence of Nozick's view in chapter 2. For other detailed and persuasive criticisms of tracking accounts of knowledge, again see Hawthorne (2003).

8   Susan Haack (1995) comes perilously close to do doing just this.

9   Sosa suggests that one must appeal at this point to pragmatic considerations. We are interested in the reliability of others precisely because we want to rely on information they provide. If we specify the relevant belief-producing processes too narrowly, the information conveyed about their epistemic "virtue" will be useless in generalizing to other situations. If too broad, it will be useless because we can't apply it to specific situations.

10   The term "internalism" is *sometimes* used in such a way that one is an internalist about knowledge provided that one is an internalist about justification.

Chapter 6

Inferential Justification

Introduction

In chapters 4 and 5 we looked at both internalist and externalist accounts of noninferential justification. Despite the fact that internalists and externalists endorse radically different accounts of noninferential justification and knowledge, both camps are committed to the view that all epistemic justification requires the existence of noninferential justification. We haven't said much yet about what, if anything, we are noninferentially justified in believing, on either traditional or externalist accounts of noninferential justification. We'll return to that question when we examine the arguments of the skeptic. But there is another critical question for metaepistemology, and that concerns the way in which one can move beyond the foundations for justification and knowledge to the rest of what we take ourselves to be justified in believing. In this chapter we will examine more closely competing accounts concerning what is required for inferential justification.

We said in chapter 3 that philosophers with radically different accounts of noninferential justification tend to agree that if one's purported justification for believing P involves inference from some other different proposition E, that justification will require that one be justified in believing E. The looming regress is eliminated with the introduction of noninferentially justified beliefs – beliefs that can legitimately terminate chains of reasoning. But it is also obvious that in order for S to be justified in believing P on the basis of E we require *more* than that S be justified in believing E and that S base the belief that P on E. I might base my belief that you will have a long life on my justified belief that you have a long "life line" on the palm of your hand, but that belief about the length of your life will still be unjustified. Why? Either because (1) there isn't an appropriate connection between the truth of the proposition that you have the long life line and the truth of the proposition that you'll live a long time or (2) you have no reason to believe that the propositions are appropriately connected. The position one takes on whether it is (1) or (2) that captures the missing condition for inferential justification is a position that defines another internalism/externalism debate – the debate I call the *inferential* internalism/externalism debate.

Inferential Internalism

The inferential internalist is committed to the view that for S to be justified in believing P on the basis of E, S must not only be justified in believing E but must also be justified in believing that E makes probable P (where E's entailing P can be viewed as the upper limit of E's making probable P). On this way of putting the inferential internalist's commitment, the key concept becomes the concept of one proposition's making probable another. Alternatively, the inferential internalist might argue that having a justified belief in P on the basis of E requires having justification for believing an epistemic principle that licenses belief in P on the basis of E. In what follows I'm going to assume that an epistemic principle will license an inference only in virtue of an appropriate relation between the content of one's premises and the content of the conclusion one infers from those premises. I'm going to assume, in other words, that the inferential internalist holds that inferential justification involves "seeing" the appropriate connection between one's premises and what one infers from those premises.

As I noted in chapter 3, it is an understatement to suggest that inferential internalism is not all that popular these days. Even philosophers attracted to the view that noninferential justification requires at least potential access to the conditions that constitute that noninferential justification shy away from the view that inferential justification requires access to the *connection* between premises and conclusion. The general view seems to be that the inferential internalist's requirements for inferential justification are too strong – that they invite either vicious regress or skepticism. One famous worry is that illustrated by Carroll's famous dialogue (1895) between the Tortoise and Achilles.[1] Paraphrasing loosely, the Tortoise doesn't see how one could ever get oneself in a position to believe the conclusion of any argument. Suppose, the Tortoise says, someone argues for Q by pointing out that it is both true that P and true that if P then Q. Won't one need some reason for supposing that those premises give one a reason to believe Q? Fatally, Achilles obliges by supplementing the premises with an additional conditional premise: If P and (if P then Q) then Q. Naturally, the Tortoise is no more satisfied than he was before. He still wants reason to think that the new collection of premises makes rational belief in Q. We can add yet another premise: (If P and (if P then Q) then Q, then Q), but, of course, if the Tortoise's original concern was legitimate, we aren't making any progress.

There is no real paradox for the inferential internalist however. While it is folly to suppose there is some need to strengthen an argument whose premises entail its conclusion by adding a premise to that effect, it is quite another matter to suppose that in order to rationally believe the conclusion of an argument based on its premises one must "see" the connection between premises and conclusion. It would, indeed, be unfortunate if the only way to discover connections between premises and conclusion is to *infer* those connections from yet other premises. That would generate a vicious regress. The moral for the inferential internalist is that there had better be some way of understanding connections between premises and conclusions that allows one to secure noninferential knowledge of the connections. We'll return to this point shortly.

Even if inferential internalism doesn't entail a vicious regress, one might still insist that one should have very good reason to accept a view that will, as we shall see, make it far more difficult to avoid skepticism. But prima facie plausible reasons to accept inferential internalism aren't that hard to come by. There seem to be all sorts of contexts in which someone's failure to have good reason to believe that there exists an appropriate connection between one's premises and one's conclusion is *sufficient* for their lacking inferential justification. In chapter 3 we talked about the palm reader who infers that someone will have a long life based on the length of the "life line" on the palm of his hand. We surely reject the palm reader's conclusion as irrational because we are convinced that the palm reader has no good reason to believe that there is a connection between the length of the palm line and the length of a life. Consider another example. The astrologer makes all sorts of predictions about your life based on your birthday and the positions of celestial bodies. Almost all of us think that the astrologer's predictions are comically irrational. Why? It is not that we doubt his knowledge of the stars. Rather, we doubt that he has any reason to believe that the positions of celestial bodies has anything to do with the affairs of human beings.

Mike Huemer (2002) has pointed out that one must be very careful relying on this sort of example in order to make plausible inferential internalism. The problem is that we often enthymematically describe our reasoning. I call the police and tell them that I've been robbed. Asked why I think that is so, I offer as my evidence that my valuables are missing, my window is broken, there are footprints both outside the window and on my carpet. In ordinary contexts, we obviously won't quarrel with the suggestion that this constitutes pretty good evidence that I've been robbed. But it is doubtful that the truths to which I appeal *in isolation* allow me to infer the conclusion. Arguably, it is only with an incredibly complex array of background information that these truths allow me to rationally reach the conclusion that I've been robbed. I know, for example, that I live in a culture in which it is not acceptable for friends to break into my house if I'm not at home to borrow valuables. I know that windows do not break for no apparent reason causing both footprints to appear in various places and valuables to disappear. I'm confident that I'm not psychotic and prone to stage robberies the staging of which I often subsequently forget. It is only against such background information that I can legitimately draw the conclusion that I've been robbed.

It is, of course, unlikely that I have explicitly and consciously entertained all of the propositions in my "background" evidence. As you will recall from earlier discussion, philosophers distinguish among the various propositions we believe those to which we give "occurrent" consent and those which we merely "dispositionally" believe. Moments before you read this sentence, you could accurately be described as someone who believes that 2 is greater than 1, that 3 is greater than 1, that 4 is greater than 1, and so on *ad infinitum*. You also believed that your toenail is smaller than the state of Alaska, the state of New York, the state of South Dakota, and so on for indefinitely many places. As we saw, it is not all that easy to give an adequate account of a dispositional belief. As a first stab, we suggested that S dispositionally believes P if S would immediately assent to P were S to consider it. But that doesn't adequately distinguish between propositions one comes to believe for the first time when one considers them and propositions one has believed "all along." Furthermore, it is an embarrassing consequence of such an account that we all dispositionally believe that we are conscious even when we are in a dreamless sleep. After all, even when we are in a dreamless sleep, it is true that if we *were* to consider the question of whether we were conscious we would reach the conclusion that we were. But even if there is no straightforward way to define dispositional belief, we are surely going to acknowledge the existence of beliefs we "carry around" with us even if we rarely bring them to the fore of consciousness. And however we understand dispositional beliefs, it is surely going to be possible to allow them a role in the way in which we reach conclusions.

These observations are relevant to evaluating the initial plausibility of the above arguments for inferential internalism. Huemer argues that where the principle seems plausible we will, on reflection, regard the description of the evidence from which we infer the conclusion as *incomplete*. We may infer that a solution is acidic from the fact that the litmus paper in the solution turned red, but we only infer that conclusion relying on some additional *premise* describing correlations between the color of litmus paper in a solution and the character of that solution. We *do* need to have reason to believe that there is a connection between litmus paper's turning red in the solution and the solution's being an acid but only because we need that *premise* in order to reach the conclusion. Both inferential internalists and inferential externalists agree, typically, that for inference to yield justified belief, we must be justified in believing the premises from which we infer our conclusion. If we are relying on a premise describing a connection between the color of litmus paper and the character of the solution in which it is placed then, to be sure, we will need reason to believe that such a connection obtains. But once we have all of the premises upon which we rely and it is true that those premises make likely the conclusion we infer from them, we do not need in addition access to the relation between premises and conclusion.

So returning to our astrologer, it might now seem plausible to suppose that no-one, not even an astrologer, thinks that a reasonable person can reach conclusions about the future based on information about celestial bodies and that information alone. Even astrologers at least implicitly recognize that they will need to rely on additional *premises* describing past correlations between the positions of planets and the affairs of people, premises which must be justifiably believed if they are to transfer their justification to some conclusion inferred from them. And whether or not the astrologer realizes this, *we* are convinced that they need justified belief in such premises in order to reach their conclusion. But that admission constitutes no concession to inferential internalism. When *all* of one's premises are justifiably believed and the argument is *good* that is sufficient to yield justified belief in the conclusion.

While Huemer is right to caution us against drawing inappropriate conclusions from thinking about enthymematic reasoning, there still seem to be strong reasons for embracing inferential internalism. Consider the most uncontroversial example of an argument with a strong connection between premises and conclusion, a deductively valid argument (an argument whose premises entail its conclusion). Suppose that I infer conclusion C from evidence E where E entails C, but the entailment is far too complicated for me to see. I am, however, *caused* to believe C when I believe E. Perhaps I was hypnotized last night and under hypnotic influence was told that I would believe C if I were to come to know E. It still seems plausible to suppose that even though I believe C based on E where E entails C, I have no epistemic reason to believe C as long as I am unable to see or even understand the way in which C entails E.

One might object that this argument relies on a controversial assumption about the basing relation. One might argue that in order for one's belief that C to be based on one's belief that E, more must be true than that the latter causes the former. But while that claim might have some credibility, I suspect it is only because we may want to build in the awareness of the connection between premises and conclusion before we will concede that the basing relation obtains. But, of course, that only strengthens the inferential internalist's position that awareness of connections between premises and conclusions is critical in securing inferential justification.

Suppose that we become convinced that inferential internalism is true. In discussing the Tortoise and Achilles we conceded that to avoid vicious regress, the inferential internalist had better find a way of understanding the relation between premises and conclusions of good arguments that would allow for the possibility of noninferential awareness of those connections. It is often conceded by traditional foundationalists that one can include in the foundations of knowledge *a priori* knowledge of certain necessary truths. One can know without inference that bachelors are unmarried, that two plus two equals four, that the opposite angles of intersecting straight lines are equal. It is also usually conceded that one can know without inference that one proposition logically entails another, at least if the entailment is relatively straightforward. One can know, for example, that the proposition that $[P$ and (if P then $Q)]$ entails Q. So there may be no particular problem satisfying the internalist's requirements for inferential justification when the inference in question is deductively valid and relatively simple. As we will see more clearly in the next chapter, however, *deduction* from available foundations probably won't take us very far from those foundations – we won't be able to use such reasoning to justify common sense beliefs about the world around us. In order to reach the conclusions we pre-philosophically take to be justified we will need to engage in reasoning that is good but not deductively valid. Put another way, we will need to rely on arguments whose premises only make highly probable their conclusions. I see dark clouds approaching and, upon recalling past experience with dark clouds and rain, infer that it will be raining soon. My evidence obviously doesn't guarantee the truth of my conclusion. Nevertheless, I might reasonably believe the conclusion based on those premises if I can "see" that the premises make probable the conclusion. But what is this relation of making probable that is supposed to hold between my premises and my conclusion? More specifically, how can we understand that relation in such a way that one can discover the relation without relying on inference?

The above discussion of entailment suggests that if we are inferential internalists we might want to develop an understanding of making probable that makes it as much like entailment as possible. Many years ago, John Maynard Keynes (1921) suggested just such a view. He claimed that the epistemologist should recognize that just as propositions can stand in relations of entailment to one another, so also they can stand in relations of making probable. Further, he argued, when one proposition makes probable another, that they stand in that relation is a necessary truth knowable *a priori* (knowable without inference). To be sure, there are important differences between making probable and entailing. When P entails Q it is absolutely impossible that P be true while Q is false. Put another way, there are no conceivable circumstances in which P is true while Q is false. From the fact that P entails Q, therefore, it follows immediately that the conjunction of P with every other proposition also entails Q. If my being a man while all men are mortal entails that I'm mortal, it follows that my being a man while all men are mortal and squirrels have bushy tails entails that I'm mortal. By contrast, it obviously isn't true that if P makes probable Q then the conjunction of P with any other information also makes probable Q. To illustrate the point we need a plausible example of the probability relation and as we will see in the next chapter there are no philosophically uncontroversial examples. But suppose, for the sake of argument, that the fact that I seem to vividly remember putting my keys on my desk makes probable that I did. Even if that is true it doesn't follow that my seeming to remember that I put the keys on my desk while discovering them in my pocket makes probable that I put them on my desk.

The concession that P might make probable Q even though (P and R) makes improbable Q should not be confused with the concession that it wasn't a necessary truth that P makes probable Q. You don't show it is possible that P doesn't make probable Q by pointing out that P can be true while Q is false. Keynes would argue that you don't even falsify the claim by pointing out that it can typically be the case that propositions like P are true while propositions like Q are false. Russell (1948, p. 212) once argued that we can make perfectly good sense of the hypothesis that we were created a moment ago replete with a vast array of "false" memory experiences of a past that didn't exist. Imagine such a possibility and ask yourself whether your memories would still make probable for you the various and sundry conclusions you reach about your past. At least some philosophers (more about this later) are convinced that in such a situation it would be wildly irrational for you not to believe the "testimony" of your memory and therefore that in the sense of making probable relevant to epistemic rationality, in such a world truths about what you seem to remember are still making probable for you truths about the past. Further reflection on the thought experiment might convince you that you can't even *imagine* having a vivid memory without that memory making at least initially probable the truth of the proposition about the past that you are so irresistibly inclined to believe. And if you reach this conclusion, you might now be inclined to think Keynes was right in supposing that there are probability connections that obtain necessarily between certain sorts of propositions.

Even if Keynes is right and there are arguments whose premises necessarily make probable their conclusions and even if he is right in supposing that we could discover those probability connections *a priori*, it doesn't follow that such discoveries would be easy. Keynesians are often criticized for particular claims about probability that turn out to be problematic. One such claim invokes the so-called Principle of Indifference. It is tempting to think that if there are two hypotheses, P and not-P, and you have no reason to choose between them, you should assign them an equal chance of being true. In this case, since they are exclusive (either P or not-P is true) we should assign them each a probability of 0.5 relative to our ignorance. But suppose the two hypotheses are that the table is brown and it is not the case that the table is brown, and that I have no evidence whatsoever concerning the particular color of the table. Intuitively, it seems wrong to assign the hypotheses an equal probability of being true. There are many more ways of being not-brown than there are of being brown. We should divide the possibilities into claims of comparable generality. The table is either brown, or black, or red, etc. Only then can we think of assigning the hypotheses equal probability.

It turns out, however, that it is not always easy to figure out how to generate the "right" comparison class of hypotheses. Paradoxes arise. Suppose, for example, that I tell you that I drove my car exactly one mile and that it took me between 1 minute and 2 minutes and thus that I was traveling somewhere between 30 mph and 60 mph. You know nothing else that bears on the situation. Intuitively, it seems plausible enough to suppose that the probability that it took me between 1 and $1\frac{1}{2}$ minutes is the same (0.5) as the probability that it took me between $1\frac{1}{2}$ and 2 minutes. It seems just as plausible, however, to suppose that the hypothesis that I was traveling between 30 mph and 45 mph and the hypothesis that I was traveling between 45 mph and 60 mph are equally likely (each has a 0.5 probability). The problem is that it seems I can't consistently assign 0.5 probability to both the hypothesis that I was traveling between 30 and 45 mph and to the hypothesis that it took me between $1\frac{1}{2}$ and 2 minutes. At 45 mph it would take me only $1\frac{1}{3}$ minutes to travel the mile. Which way of dividing up the possibilities is correct?[2]

Consider another now familiar puzzle of probability, the Monty Hall puzzle (named after the game show host who apparently actually raised it with mathematicians). On Monty Hall's game show, contestants would get themselves in a position where they had to choose between three doors, door #1, door #2 and door #3. They knew there was a valuable prize behind one of the doors and nothing of value behind the other two. After the contestant chose, say, door #1, Monty Hall would typically open one of the other doors (say, door #3) to show that it had nothing of value behind it. He would then ask the contestant if she wanted to stick with her original choice or to switch to door #2. The vast majority of people will conclude that the contestant had no reason to switch. It seems obvious to most people that, relative to her new information, it is just as likely that the prize is behind #1 as it is behind #2. But it isn't! The rational strategy is to switch. It is now twice as likely for her that the prize is behind door #2. (To convince yourself that this is so just keep thinking about the fact that "switchers" win in these scenarios every time they picked wrong initially – something that happens 2 out of 3 times.)

The moral to draw, however, is not that there is a problem with Keynes's conception of probability. Rather, it may show only that one can easily make a mistake and think that there is a probability connection between propositions when there isn't. It doesn't follow that there aren't necessary truths about probability connections between premises and conclusions that are knowable *a priori*. On some views, all of mathematics consists of necessary truths knowable *a priori*. Even if such a view is true it doesn't follow, as we sadly learned in our math finals, that such truths are *easy* to know.

Inferential Externalism

The inferential externalist is convinced that the inferential internalist's requirements for inferential justification are far too strong. It is enough that there be the appropriate connection between premises and conclusions for one to get a justified belief in one's conclusion based on justified belief in one's premises. While the inferential externalist wouldn't need to abandon a Keynesian view of epistemic probability, the vast majority propose a quite different account of how one can acquire justified belief through inference.

In discussing noninferential justification, we looked at a number of externalist accounts of such justification. Each of those accounts offers an analogous way of understanding inferential justification. But the view that will interest us most here is the extension of the reliabilist's analysis to inferential justification. The parallel account of inferential justification suggested by the causal theorist would simply recognize that the causal connections that extend from the feature of the world that makes true a belief (in the simplest case) and the belief it makes true can involve links that are themselves other beliefs. Most causal theorists will insist that if these intermediary beliefs are to secure knowledge of the relevant output belief, they themselves will need to be justified. But the extension of the causal theory is most at home with an account of inferential knowledge rather than justified belief. On at least one natural understanding of inferential justification, possessing inferential justification for believing some proposition P is perfectly compatible with P's being false. The causal connections that it might have been plausible to require as the source of a very strong, indeed infallible, noninferential justification, are too strong to require for justification in general.

In precisely the same way, tracking accounts of knowledge can certainly recognize a distinction between beliefs that track their truth makers in the relevant way without the tracking mechanism involving other justified beliefs, and beliefs that track the relevant truth makers in part by virtue of a tracking mechanism that employs other justified beliefs. But again, as Nozick himself admits, the tracking account is most at home as an account of knowledge. When we are trying to understand justified belief, it seems obvious that we require far too much of justified belief if we require it to track its truth maker. As we noted above, we want to allow for the possibility of justified false belief. And when a belief is false it obviously isn't tracking the truth.

Reliabilist accounts of inferential justification

As we saw, the reliabilist offers an account of noninferential justification that allows for a noninferentially justified belief to be false. Indeed, one might possess noninferential justification for believing some proposition when the justification is not very strong at all. The belief-independent, unconditionally reliable process that produces the belief might be such that it would result in true beliefs only barely more than 50 percent of the time. The reliabilist will have no difficulty in principle, then, extending the account of fallible noninferential justification to fallible inferential justification.

You will recall that the central idea behind reliabilism is that we could understand justified belief as belief produced in a reliable way. On the crudest view, a belief is produced reliably when it was produced in a way that usually results in true belief. [The base clause of the reliabilist's recursive foundationalist analysis of justification identifies noninferentially justified beliefs with those that are produced by belief-independent, unconditionally reliable processes.] A process is belief-independent when its "input" is something other than belief. The justified beliefs we acquire that way can in turn give us premises from which we can infer still other truths. In the language favored by the reliabilist, we can recognize the existence of belief-dependent, conditionally reliable processes. A belief-producing process is belief-dependent when its "input" includes at least some beliefs. And such a process is *conditionally* reliable when its "output" beliefs would usually be true *provided that its input beliefs were true.* [The output beliefs of belief-dependent, conditionally reliable processes are inferentially justified when the relevant input beliefs are themselves justified. These beliefs or some causal ancestors of these beliefs must be non-inferentially justified.]

So consider an example of a conditionally reliable belief-forming process par excellence – valid deduction. Suppose as a result of believing P and (if P then Q) I come to believe Q. My "programming" always takes me from the belief that P and the belief that if P then Q to the belief that Q. The process is 100 percent conditionally reliable. When I form true input beliefs like P and (if P then Q) and my output belief is Q, my output belief is true 100 percent of the time. If there are non-deductive patterns of inference that get me to the truth more often than not when my input beliefs are true, those processes will have a conditional reliability somewhere between 50 percent and 100 percent. Just as the reliabilist would insist that a belief might be noninferentially justified even if the believer has no idea how the belief was formed, so also the reliabilist will insist that a belief might be inferentially justified even if the believer has no idea of what the belief-dependent process producing the belief is and has no reason to suppose that the process in question is conditionally reliable.

We saw in the last chapter that reliabilism has a great deal of attraction for philosophers desperate to avoid skepticism. If the view were true, then, provided that evolution and nature co-operate, we may have many more noninferentially justified beliefs than traditional foundationalists allowed. Indeed, any belief could in principle be noninferentially justified. With a bit of imagination we can imagine some unconditionally reliable, belief-independent process that produces my belief that God exists, that the stock market will go up, or that there is life on the planet Neptune. We also had occasion to worry that possessing the kind of noninferential justification defined by the reliabilist (or other paradigm externalists) might not have much to do with the kind of assurance we might have supposed that justification should provide. Furthermore, it seemed that we can imagine indistinguishable non-veridical counterparts of what we take our actual situation to be, situations in which many think it obvious that the justificatory status of those beliefs should be unaltered even though reliabilism seems to commit one to a quite different conclusion. In addition to these general worries, we noted that the reliabilist faces more detailed objections concerning the specification of the relevant belief-forming processes. The virtues and alleged vices of the reliabilist's account of noninferential justification all have parallels with the reliabilist's account of inferential justification. To show this, we need only alter the various thought experiments to stipulate this time that the process under consideration is a belief-dependent process. Indeed, to illustrate this point we need only postulate that some of the belief-forming processes we supposed, in the last chapter, to be belief-independent are actually belief-dependent.

Consider, for example, beliefs about the past based on memory. Now it is not at all clear whether beliefs resulting from memory are typically beliefs that result from belief-independent or belief-dependent processes (as the reliabilist understands the distinction). It is entirely possible that we find ourselves believing certain propositions about the past without in any sense first contemplating the fact that we seem to remember having had certain experiences. But it's also possible that at least sometimes we actually notice that we have some vivid memory experience and subsequently form a belief based on that experience. In such situations, it is entirely plausible to suppose that the belief so formed results from a belief-dependent process. So suppose I become aware of my seeming to remember that I had a headache this morning and consciously infer from that apparent memory that I had a headache. Again, we have the problem of specifying precisely what the process is. To be sure, it can be characterized as an inference from seeming to remember an experience to the conclusion that the experience occurred. It can also be described as my becoming aware of my *vividly* seeming to remember something and as a result coming to believe that the experience occurred. Yet again, it might be described as an inference to a past experience from a proposition describing a vivid memory experience when that memory experience occurs in the mind of a philosopher whose memory never was that good and who isn't getting any younger. All might be quite accurate descriptions of the inference in question, but we may get quite different assessments of the reliability of the process depending on how it is characterized.

Still, assuming for the sake of argument that we sometimes do actually infer truths about the past from truths we notice about apparent memory, we need to decide what to say about the possible situation in which we were created, unbeknownst to us, a few moments ago replete with vivid but massively misleading apparent memories of a fictitious past. It seems that the reliabilist is committed to the view that the beliefs we would form about our past result from a (conditionally) unreliable belief-forming process and thus should be unjustified. But our intuitions here will be precisely what they were when we considered the same thought experiment under the supposition that memory-induced beliefs about the past were beliefs produced by a belief-independent process. It's very hard for the traditional epistemologist to see what could make it the case that our inhabitants of this bizarre world were epistemically irrational for believing (falsely) what they do about their past. They surely had every reason to believe precisely what we believe. A person who perversely infers that some experience didn't occur because they seemed to remember its occurring would have the rational belief, according to the reliabilist! But many of us are strongly inclined to think that the perversity I just described is an epistemic perversity – the person would be flying in the face of the evidence.

Lastly, the reliabilist's account of inferential justification leaves us with what some would take to be an odd disconnect between possessing justification and having some sort of assurance of truth. Suppose that I'm in the habit of inferring that there is a god who is angry about something from the proposition that there is lightning in the sky. Suppose further that the Greeks had it almost right. There are Olympian-style gods, one of whom is the god of thunder and lightning, and that god lets the bolts loose when he is ticked off about something. If I were living in such a world my beliefs would be inferentially justified. But now suppose, again, that I'm becoming philosophically reflective. I've encountered a number of intellectuals who have been ridiculing me for my bizarre habit of making inferences about gods from my observations of what they take to be perfectly mundane natural phenomena. They are beginning to shake my confidence a bit even though I can't rid myself of what they take to be a very odd belief-forming habit. In the sense in which I am anxious to put my beliefs on a firm footing – the sense in which I am anxious to get assurance that the god I take to be responsible for the lightning actually exists – am I getting that assurance from the fact that I have a reliably produced belief? The answer seems obviously "No," and again the inferential internalist has an explanation of why that answer is correct. Assurance comes only from "seeing" the relevant connection between our premises and our conclusions.

Mixed Views and Derivative Concepts of Inferential Justification

However plausible inferential internalism might seem, the fact remains that it does seem to require a great deal for a belief to be inferentially justified. That, coupled with the meager foundations that most internalist accounts of noninferential justification allow, makes it difficult to reconcile the view with the way in which we casually distinguish between rational and irrational beliefs. I take a drink of water and expect it to quench my thirst. Is that expectation rational? Before we get immersed in metaepistemological controversies, it certainly seems a prime candidate for a rational belief. But it doesn't seem a very good candidate for a non-inferentially justified belief on the acquaintance theory. It hardly seems plausible to suppose that I am directly acquainted with some future state of affairs – my thirst's being quenched. So if it is a rational expectation, it is presumably because I can legitimately infer that proposition from some body of propositions I justifiably believe. But what precisely is the body of evidence on which I rely? Is it the fact that I seem to remember many occasions on which I drank water before when it quenched my thirst? That's the answer many philosophers give, but if we are honest it might strike us as involving gross over-intellectualization if it is intended to be a description of any actual conscious inference I run through. Certainly, if you ask me, I might be able to dredge up in my memory some specific occasions on which I had a cool drink of water that quenched my thirst, but as I get older and my memory gets worse I might not be all that confident that I am remembering correctly the occasions on which I engaged in this behavior.

And consider again perceptual beliefs about the external world. As we'll see in the next chapter, it is difficult to argue within the framework of the acquaintance theory that we are directly acquainted with any features of the physical world. But if we must infer the existence of the familiar objects surrounding us from some truths noninferentially known, what precisely is that body of evidence upon which we rely? The radical empiricist had a ready answer. If rational, our beliefs about the physical world must be inferred from what we know about fleeting, subjective sensations.[3] We are directly acquainted with the fact that we seem to see something square and brown and from our direct knowledge of the proposition made true by that fact we infer the existence of a square brown object. The question of how we can legitimately infer that conclusion from the alleged available evidence is important (and will be addressed further in the next chapter). But there is a preliminary challenge one might raise. If we pay close attention to what we actually do when we form beliefs about the world around us, it is a bit difficult to convince ourselves that we actually first pay attention to subjective appearances, and then from what we know about those appearances come to conclusions about the nature of an external reality. It is already a bit of a stretch to describe ourselves as having *beliefs* about our physical surroundings. It is more that we simply have certain expectations that things will be so and so, expectations that we become aware of primarily when we are surprised. It takes a great deal of effort, the kind of effort that painters, for example, expend, even to concentrate on how things look rather than how we take things to be.

Earlier we distinguished dispositional beliefs from occurrent beliefs. It is certainly possible that we harbor all sorts of dispositional beliefs about the character of our subjective experience. We might even harbor dispositional beliefs in propositions asserting that those appearances make probable certain truths about our physical environment. But it is just as likely, one might suppose, that we have evolved in such a way that experience causes us to form beliefs about our environment without our needing to take account of those experiences through judgments about their occurrence. If the inferential internalist is correct, and if we are simply determined through our evolutionary history to believe certain propositions as a result of sensory stimulation, have we no choice but to concede that such beliefs are unjustified? And is this conclusion not simply implausible given the fact that we don't hesitate to characterize such beliefs as paradigmatically rational?

It is certainly open to the internalists in general, and inferential internalists in particular, to concede that we often allow as justified beliefs that fail to satisfy the philosophically stringent criteria they set out. Internalists might allow that the kind of epistemic justification they are primarily concerned with is a kind of *ideal* justification – the kind of justification philosophers pursue in attempting to satisfy philosophical curiosity. In ordinary contexts, we will often settle for something short of ideal justification in our efforts to distinguish rational and irrational beliefs. In short, we might allow derivative concepts of epistemically justified beliefs. Suppose, for example, that someone S is caused to believe some proposition P by the fact that he has had certain experiences (let's call that fact E). Suppose further that there is in fact a probabilistic connection between the proposition E (the proposition made true by the fact that E) and P, or more likely that there is a probabilistic connection between the proposition E together with background information S possesses and P. By hypothesis, S doesn't even contemplate the proposition that E, nor, consequently, does S entertain the assertion that E makes probable P. From at least one (epistemic) point of view, being the kind of person whose beliefs are caused in this way is certainly better than being the kind of person whose belief is caused by features of the world that are not the truth-makers for propositions that could be employed in rational inference. We might, therefore, allow that S's belief is in a sense epistemically rational even if it falls short of ideal epistemic rationality.

In allowing that a belief might be at least derivatively rational in virtue of having the relevant causal origin, it might seem that our hypothetical internalist is coming close to adopting the reliabilist's view. After all, the cornerstone of reliabilism is the alleged insight that if a belief is caused in the right way that belief can be justified even if the believer has little insight into the nature of the causal origin. There is, however, one critical difference. On the view sketched briefly above, the derivative epistemic status of the belief can still be viewed as a function of those Keynesian probabilistic connections holding between propositions. My belief that P is justified (derivatively) when it is caused by some fact that makes true a proposition E, where E makes probable P. On this view, we can still allow that the victims of demonic machinations, who posed such a problem for reliabilists and their externalist companions, have beliefs with precisely the same justificatory status as the inhabitants of the world in which we think we live.

Suggested readings

Alston, William. 1989. "An Internalist Externalism," in *Epistemic Justification*. Ithaca: Cornell University Press.

Huemer, Mike. 2002. "Fumerton's Principle of Inferential Justification." *Journal of Philosophical Research*, 27, 329–40.

Russell, Bertrand. 1959. *The Problems of Philosophy*, chapters 6 and 11. Oxford: Oxford University Press.

Notes

1 I thank Jim Van Cleve for helpful discussion relating to this point.
2 As Tim McGrew pointed out to me, Keynes himself urged great caution in attempts to apply a principle of indifference.
3 Less radical empiricists will expand the available evidence to include apparent memories and expectations that occupy present consciousness – still subjective and fleeting.

Chapter 7

Metaepistemology and Skepticism

Introduction

It would be no exaggeration to suggest that a good part of the history of epistemology has been shaped by the looming presence of the skeptic. We have already seen his shadow in our discussion of the way in which epistemologists modify analyses of knowledge in an attempt to avoid being forced to reject too much of what we commonly claim to know. Epistemologists have been struggling to respond to the arguments of the skeptic for literally thousands of years. That is not to say that there has been anything like a uniform response. Indeed, while some philosophers consider skepticism a legitimate view that deserves to be taken seriously, other philosophers are quite candid in admitting that they will reject out of hand any view that leads to skepticism. Even these philosophers, however, are often heavily influenced by the skeptic. Their epistemological views are shaped largely by this determination to avoid skepticism. In this chapter I want to re-examine the structure of classical skeptical arguments and look at the way in which the internalism/externalism debate discussed in the last two chapters will bear on how one might respond to those arguments. As we shall see, the prospects for avoiding skepticism are certainly brighter within the framework of an externalist epistemology. But as we have already hinted, there is a potential price the externalist pays if one expects justification to carry with it assurance of the sort the skeptic sought.

Kinds of Skepticism

There are many varieties of skepticism. In the first instance we can distinguish between skeptics concerning the possibility of *knowledge* and skeptics concerning the possibility of epistemically *rational* belief. Within both knowledge skepticism and rational belief skepticism, we can distinguish *global* and *local* versions.

Global Skepticism

The global skeptic with respect to knowledge claims that we don't know, or stronger still, *cannot* know any truth. The global skeptic with respect to epistemically rational belief claims that we have no epistemically rational beliefs, or stronger still, that we *cannot* have any epistemically rational beliefs. This last view is the strongest of all skepticisms and it is, understandably, difficult to find proponents of the view. Strong global skepticism with respect to rational belief has some very odd features indeed. For one thing, the view is epistemically self-refuting. Let us say that a view is epistemically self-refuting when the truth of the view entails that one has no reason whatsoever to believe it. If this strong form of skepticism is true, it trivially follows that its proponent has no reason whatsoever to believe it. And it is tempting to infer from this that the view needn't be taken seriously. This conclusion, however, might be a bit hasty. It is not clear that one can simply dismiss the arguments for a view on the grounds that if the view is true one could have no reason to think that the arguments for it are good. One might still be in the unfortunate position of believing the skeptic's premises and believing that the premises of those arguments imply their conclusions.

An example might be useful. When I was a child I had a magic eight ball. The idea was that you ask the magic ball a question that can be answered either "Yes" or "No," shake the ball, and see what answer floats to the transparent glass opening on the face of the ball. Now suppose we lived in a society that took eight-ball reasoning very seriously indeed. Our society is, however, plagued by a few skeptics with respect to eight-ball reasoning. They think reaching conclusions this way is barmy. Unfazed, you decide to test eight-ball reasoning by asking the eight ball whether it can be relied upon to arrive at the truth. You shake it and to your consternation you discover that the answer that floats to the surface is "No." Worried that this might be an aberration, you shake it again and still get the answer "No." On the verge of abandoning the eight ball as an indicator of truth, you suddenly realize that if eight ball reasoning is defective we can't use it to conclude that it is defective. Confidently, you continue using the eight ball to discover truth.

Obviously, something has gone seriously wrong here. Certainly, if it is true that eight-ball reasoning is defective, you can't use that reasoning to reach the conclusion that it is. But you are surely not off the hook as an eight-ball reasoner. You've got serious problems. In precisely the same way, if the skeptic can come up with an argument whose premises you accept and whose premises you believe yield a radical skeptical conclusion, it does follow that either the conclusion is false or you don't have reason to believe that the argument is good. But you are not off the hook either. You still need to deal with the fact that you have a belief system that seems to you to entail radical skepticism.

The global skeptic with respect to knowledge doesn't face quite the same problems of epistemic self-refutation. To be sure, if it is true that we don't know anything, it follows that we don't know that we don't know anything. But we might still have good reason to believe that we don't know anything. The reasons might fall short of what is required for knowledge.

Local Skepticism

As I implied above, there are almost no global skeptics with respect to epistemically rational belief. And there are few global skeptics with respect to knowledge. The most influential skeptics have typically been local skeptics. A local skeptic with respect to knowledge claims that we don't know some *class* of propositions. A local skeptic with respect to epistemically rational belief claims that we don't have epistemic reasons to believe some *class* of propositions. To be sure, you are only going to get philosophical notoriety as a skeptic if the class of propositions you target with your skepticism is one that most people think they do know or rationally believe. So you might be a local knowledge skeptic with respect to theories purporting to explain the extinction of the dinosaurs. But you won't join the ranks of the great philosophical skeptics with that rather common sense caution about accepting theories that have been under constant attack since they have been proposed. The philosophically interesting skepticisms have attacked the possibility of knowing or rationally believing any proposition describing the physical world, or the past, or other minds, or the future, or the "unobservable" theoretical entities postulated by science.

In what follows I want to examine local skepticism with respect to rational belief. In chapter 2, we saw that it is difficult to avoid endorsing very strong requirements for knowledge. It is distressingly easy to get students in our introductory philosophy courses to simply shrug their shoulders with a resigned "Well, what did you expect?" when confronted with skeptical challenges concerning the possibility of knowing with absolute certainty even the most commonplace of truths. Their distress level picks up considerably, however, when what is challenged is the possibility of even rational belief in that which they have always taken for granted. I'm not suggesting that knowledge skepticism is uninteresting. Rather, I'm suggesting that we might be quite happy if in the face of relentless assault from the skeptics we could at least salvage the conclusion that we have rational belief. As we saw, on variations of the justified true belief account of knowledge, whether or not a justified belief will count as knowledge may depend simply on whether or not the world "co-operates." The most we can do is ensure that our beliefs are rational.

The Pattern of Skeptical Arguments

There is a pattern to most skeptical arguments. The skeptic begins by driving a logical wedge between the evidence available to a person and the truth of the proposition under skeptical attack. Put another way, the skeptic first tries to convince you that the justification, if any, you possess for believing what you do is at least consistent with your belief's being false. You can conceive of having the kind of justification you have even if what you believe on the basis of that justification is not true. If the skeptic's first premise is true, then it follows that we cannot deduce the proposition we think we rationally believe from the evidence at our disposal. If we accept "Cartesian" standards for knowledge, that is, if we accept the idea that knowledge requires having justification that eliminates the conceivability of error, then we may already be positioned to conclude that we don't know the proposition under skeptical attack. But if the skeptic's goal is the more radical conclusion that we have no epistemic reason at all to believe the proposition under skeptical attack, the next step in the argument is to call into question the availability of legitimate *non-deductive* reasoning to reach the conclusion in question. The precise nature of this skeptical attack will vary depending on how the skeptic's foe attempts to characterize the nature of the probabilistic reasoning.

An Illustration: The Problems of Perception

The above discussion was highly abstract. Let's illustrate the idea with a famous problem in the history of epistemology – the problem of perception. We take ourselves to be justified in believing all sorts of claims about our physical surroundings. As Descartes famously argued, the justification we have for such assertions is presumably never any better than the "testimony" of our senses when we take ourselves to be directly before "bread-box-sized" objects under favorable conditions of perception. Everything we believe about the physical world can be traced ultimately to beliefs that rely on "direct" sensory experience of our surroundings. When we reach some conclusion about the distant past based on what we read in books, for example, we rely on visual experience to conclude that the words really are there on the page.

In his famous *Meditations*, Descartes initially argued that the best justification we could possibly imagine for beliefs about our physical environment never *guarantees* the truth of what we believe. No matter how vivid our sensations seem, we can imagine having sensations indistinguishable from these in the course of a vivid dream. Alternatively, we can imagine having those sensations as a result of the machinations of an evil demon. More modern skeptical scenarios (as they are called) often appeal to possibilities suggested by what we take to be the empirical discoveries of cognitive science. If the world is as we believe it to be, the immediate cause of all of our sensations are brain states. Because we believe that, we can make perfectly good sense of movies like the cult classic *Total Recall* or *The Matrix*. The basic plot line of such films involves the idea that we could be the victims of massive hallucinatory experience indistinguishable from the experience we take to be veridical. In both movies, the intelligibility of the plot is no more problematic than the intelligibility of a machine that is capable of manipulating the brain so as to produce the very brain states that we take to be the immediate cause of our mental states. Relying on the intelligibility of these sorts of possibilities, the skeptic concludes that the justification we have for believing what we do about our physical environment never guarantees the truth of what we believe. Our justification doesn't entail the truth of what we believe.

Now on certain models of noninferential justification, the fact that our justification for accepting descriptions of our physical environment is consistent with the falsity of those beliefs implies that the justification, if any, that we possess is inferential. On an acquaintance theory of noninferential justification, you will recall, I would be noninferentially justified in believing that there is in front of me a red, round object only if I were directly acquainted with the fact that makes true that belief. But since the justification I have now is the same as the justification I would possess were I vividly hallucinating the red, round object, it seems to follow that the justification I possess now is not my direct acquaintance with the fact that a red, round object exists. After all, we need only suppose that in the indistinguishable hallucinatory experience there is no red, round object there, and hence no relation of acquaintance that I bear to that object. As we will see, the plausibility of this conclusion will be challenged on other models of noninferential justification.

Once the skeptic establishes that we don't have foundational knowledge of truths about our physical environment, the skeptic turns to the possibility of our having inferential justification. Suppose we concede that if we can justify our belief that there is a certain object in front of us, it is only through our ability to legitimately infer the existence of that object from what we know about something else. The way in which skeptics characterize the foundational truths available as evidence varies dramatically. Some argue that in all experience, both veridical and nonveridical, we are directly aware of an object, sometimes called a sense datum, that is not a physical object but that has properties of various sorts and whose existence might be taken as an indicator that a physical object lurks nearby. Other philosophers prefer what they take to be a more neutral vocabulary to describe that which we are supposed to know unproblematically. So some suggest that whether or not we actually (veridically) see a physical object that is red and round, we can say that it appears to us as if there is something red and round, or that we seem to see something red and round. (The "appears" or "seems" locution is intended to emphasize that the object might not exist. As we ordinarily use the expression "see," to claim that one actually sees an X is to imply that X exists). That language is itself potentially misleading. As Sellars (1963) and others have pointed out, we often use the language of appearing to express tentative belief (e.g. that appears to be/seems to be/looks as if it is Fred), or to describe the fact that something looks the way physical objects of a certain sort look under normal conditions (e.g. that shirt looks red, in the sense that it looks the way red things look under normal conditions). The philosopher looking for a secure foundation for empirical beliefs intends the language of appearing or seeming to be a way of describing the familiar character of the experience we have whether or not the object we take to be its cause really exists. To avoid any confusion on this point, the suggestion is sometimes made that we adopt a kind of technical (and aesthetically odd) language to describe the "phenomenal" character of experience (the character of experience of which one is directly and immediately aware). Using this technical terminology we can say that whether or not the red round object is there, we are appeared to redly and roundly. The theory underlying this choice of description is sometimes called the adverbial theory to emphasize that there might be no *object* of any sort that we are aware of in nonveridical perceiving. Rather there is just a way of sensing, a way described by the artificially constructed adverb.[1]

For the sake of this discussion let's adopt the language of seeming to perceive in order to describe the sensory state that the skeptic concedes exists but is not supposed to entail the existence of a physical object. So we are supposed to know that we seem to see something red and round, but we also know that this fact is consistent with any number of hypotheses concerning the cause of the visual sensation. What reason is there, the skeptic asks, for supposing that this visual sensation makes likely the common sense hypothesis that there is a red, round physical object causally responsible for it? Notice that the classical skeptic here is probably just taking for granted the plausibility of inferential internalism. In the absence of any reason for supposing that there is a probabilistic connection between sensations of this sort and the existence of physical objects, we simply have no reason to suppose that the object in question exists. Alternatively, the skeptic could be construed as arguing only that in the absence of reason to believe that there is the relevant probabilistic connection we have no reason to believe that we have reason to believe that the object exists.

How might we answer the skeptic? Hume (1888, p. 212) famously suggested that there is only one way to establish the existence of one kind of thing as evidence for the existence of another kind of thing, and that is to have established through past observations a correlation between the two. So, for example, if we set aside our skeptical worries for the moment, and ask ourselves why we take the dark clouds we see in the sky to be an indicator that it will probably soon rain, it is not hard to convince ourselves that the reason is that we have observed in the past a correlation between dark clouds and rain. We expect the next drink of water to quench our thirst and not kill us because we remember indefinitely many occasions upon which we drank water that quenched our thirst. This kind of reasoning is sometimes called enumerative induction: All (or most) of the F's we have observed have been G and we infer from that that the next F we encounter will be G as well, or, if we feel lucky, we might infer a generalization: that all/most F's are G's.

So, can we use inductive reasoning to establish that our subjective, fleeting sensations are reliable indicators of the physical objects we unreflectively take to be their cause? The prospects seem dim. If you claim to have discovered that in the past sensations like these were usually caused by red, round objects, the skeptic will want to know just exactly how that discovery was made. In the past did you notice that you were having a certain visual experience and then stop to find out whether the experience was veridical? Did you peak out from behind the "veil" of experience to get an experience-independent "look" at the way things are? There is no access to the world other than the access we have through sense experience. You can correlate sensations with sensations. You can discover that usually visual sensations of certain sorts, when accompanied by sensations of bodily movement (seeming to see and feel your hand approach the object) are accompanied by tactile sensations (seeming to feel a certain surface). But neither you nor anyone else could possibly correlate sensations with physical objects. You can't, Hume concluded, inductively establish sensations as probabilistic indicators of physical objects. Because Hume thought that inductive reasoning was your only hope, he seemed to embrace a fairly radical skepticism.

There are all sorts of responses to the Humean argument. Some would suggest that even if we can't establish the existence of physical objects relying on inductive reasoning, there are alternative argument forms available to refute the skeptic. Perhaps, for example, we can employ an argument to the best explanation. The American philosopher Peirce (1938) contrasted induction with what he called abduction, or reasoning to the best explanation. We find the fossilized remains of fish embedded in rock far from any source of water. We seek an explanation for this surprising phenomenon and tentatively embrace the most obvious – that the sea once covered the land.[2] The argument form seems to be something like this:

1 O (some observation of a phenomenon we want explained)
2 T would best explain O

Therefore,

3 T

Arguments of this sort seem to presuppose at the very least that it is likely that there are causal explanations for phenomena and that we have some sense of what makes one explanation better than another. Let's not worry about the first presupposition, but turn our attention to the second. How do we decide which of competing explanations for some phenomenon is the most plausible? Well, let's look at a mundane example. I see human-shaped footprints on the beach and take the best explanation of that fact to be that people walked on the beach recently. There are, of course, other hypotheses which, if true, would also explain the phenomenon. If a cow wearing boots had walked the beach recently there would also be footprints on the beach. If aliens hovering low in their spacecrafts used lasers to cut footprint-shaped marks in the beach, there would be such footprints. What makes the people hypothesis more plausible than either the cow or the alien hypothesis? The most obvious answer is that we know through past experience that footprints are usually produced by people. But if we are critically relying on that information, we should suspect that our so-called reasoning to the best explanation is really just a disguised form of inductive reasoning. Relying on an observed correlation between footprints and their causes, we conclude from a fresh case of observed footprints that they have that familiar cause. But if in general, reasoning to the best explanation collapses into inductive reasoning it will be of no help in answering the skeptic.

It would be more than a little hasty to infer from one example that reasoning to the best explanation collapses into inductive reasoning. But whatever criteria one advances for preferring one explanation to another, one will surely need to know just what makes those criteria plausible. Are simple explanations generally to be preferred to more complex explanations? There is a sense in which the answer to that question is probably "Yes." Suppose, for example, that we start with two competing explanations *H1* and *H2*, and that they have roughly equal probability of being true. I'm not sure, for example, whether it is Smith or Jones who committed the murder – the evidence doesn't seem to favor the one hypothesis over the other. Further experience, however, requires that we add some additional hypothesis to *H2* (call it *A1*). In our example, an eyewitness turns up claiming that Jones was not at the scene of the crime. To suppose that Jones is the murderer I would need to suppose that the eyewitness is lying. It is a well-accepted and common sense feature of probability theory that the probability of a conjunction (*P* and *Q*) is the probability of each conjunct multiplied (when the conjuncts are probabilistically independent.) So if the probability of *P* is 0.5 and the probability of *Q* is 0.5, the probability of it being the case that both *P* and *Q* are true is only 0.25. In our example, if *H1* and *H2* were tied prior to our needing an additional hypothesis added to *H2*, then *H1* will presumably now be more plausible than the more complex (*H2* and *A1*). In our example, Smith has a better chance of being the murderer than Jones given my new evidence. This all presupposes, however, that we had some antecedent probabilities that attached to *H1* and *H2*. In general, it is not clear how to assign these antecedent probabilities. Nor is it always clear which of two hypotheses should be viewed as more complex.

Consider, for example, the famous controversy raised by the idealist Berkeley. Berkeley (1954) advanced the suggestion that our sensations (he called them our "ideas"), were caused directly by God. He observed that it seems that we are not the author of our own sensations (as we cannot control them at will). Still, he suggested, we do know that minds are the kinds of things capable of causing mental states – we are, after all, the author of ideas in our imagination. Therefore, if we are searching for the best and simplest explanation for the fact that we have other mental states (sensations) we should choose the hypothesis that they come to us in an ordered and coherent fashion arranged by a very powerful being (God). It is an understatement to say that Berkeley's suggestion was not greeted with a great deal of enthusiasm, but if we are choosing among alternative explanations on the basis of simplicity, it is not clear that Berkeley's hypothesis would lose. After all, Berkeley recognized only two kinds of things, minds and ideas (again, where "idea" was his broad term for virtually all mental states). The materialist (as he called those who insist that the causes of sensations were material things – mind-independent objects with causal powers) posits minds, ideas, *and* material things. To be sure, Berkeley was committed to the existence of a mind quite different from the minds of finite human beings, but is a view according to which there are quite different sorts of minds as well as ideas more complex than a view that posits minds, ideas, and mind-independent material objects?

The question of whether one can muster a plausible argument from the best explanation to save the view of "common sense" is a most complex matter to which we cannot do justice here. Suffice it to say, the battle will be difficult. It is particularly important to realize that to save common sense, the hypotheses we unreflectively accept must be more likely to be true than the disjunction of all other possible explanations (all other explanations joined by "or"'s). If there are ten suspects in a murder trial, you cannot convict suspect 1 on the grounds that he was more likely to have committed the crime than each of the other suspects. That can be true even if it is much more likely that one or another of the other suspects is guilty (just as the favorite to win the Kentucky Derby is rarely actually likely to win).

Inductive reasoning and reasoning to the best explanation are only two candidates for legitimate non-deductive reasoning that might take us from the world of subjective and fleeting appearance to the world of mind-independent enduring objects. As was noted earlier, at least some philosophers make no bones about the fact that they will recognize whatever principles of reasoning they need to recognize in order to avoid skepticism. So one can simply assert that the fact that one seems to see something red and round makes likely that there is something red and round.

The principle is offered as one of indefinitely many legitimate non-deductive principles of reasoning that sanction the inferences we take to be intuitively reasonable.

If one attempts to refute skepticism by letting epistemic principles proliferate, the skeptic presupposing inferential internalism will insist that we get some plausible account of how we can discover these epistemic principles. As we saw in our discussion of inferential internalism, if one accepts the principle of inferential justification from within a foundationalist framework, we need to end not just one, but many potentially vicious infinite regresses. To be justified in believing P on the basis of $E1$ we will need to be justified in believing $E1$. We might infer that from something else, $E2$, which we infer from something else, $E3$, and so on, but we must eventually find a "foundation" for our justification in something we can justifiably believe without inference. But according to the inferential internalist, we must also be justified in believing that $E1$ makes probable P. To be sure, we might infer that from some other proposition $F1$, which we infer from some other proposition $F2$, and so until we secure a foundational end to that chain of reasoning. But that will still leave us with the task of discovering a justification for our belief that $F1$ makes likely that $E1$ makes likely P. In short, if inferential internalism is true, then there must be some propositions of the form 'E makes probable P' that we can believe with noninferential justification. On the Keynesian view of probability, there are necessary truths of the form 'E makes probable P,' truths that we can know in the same way that we can know that one proposition entails another. The Keynesian view is the only hope for the philosopher trying to avoid skepticism within the framework of a foundationalism that accepts inferential internalism.

Another Illustration: The Problem of Memory

We illustrated the classical pattern of skeptical argument with the famous problem of perception. It might be useful to provide one other brief illustration of this type of argument – the problem of justifying beliefs about the past. You think you know what you had for breakfast this morning – corn flakes. In this context, let's not worry about distinguishing between your subjective experience of eating corn flakes and your actually eating the corn flakes. What is your justification for believing that you ate the corn flakes? It's tempting to suppose that after you get over the shock of being asked this rather odd question, you might reply somewhat indignantly that you remember eating the corn flakes. As we saw in our discussion of "factive" states, verbs like "remember" are like perceptual verbs. In saying that you remember doing *X* you probably commit yourself to the truth of the claim that you did *X*. So to avoid begging the question against the skeptic, you might reply more cautiously that at the very least you seem to remember eating the corn flakes.

Can you seem to remember doing something that you didn't do? Of course. If you need any convincing, wait until you get to be my age. All those arguments marshaled by the skeptic to convince you that you could seem to see something that wasn't there can be deployed to convince you that you can seem to remember having done something you didn't do. The skeptic will have no difficulty completing the first stage in his argument – exploiting a logical gap between available evidence and the conclusion you reach about the past on the basis of that evidence. How, then, can we justify our common sense belief that memory is a reliable indicator of past events? Again, the skeptic, taking for granted inferential internalism, will assume that if you can't justify your belief in the probability claim, you have no reason to believe what you do about your breakfast. But this time the options are so incredibly stark. Any argument you try to give for the reliability of memory will surely appeal to *past* experience. Reasoning *itself* takes time and to "keep" in mind whatever premises you gather you will need to rely again on memory. But the skeptic will not allow you to use memory in your defense of the conclusion that memory is reliable. You wouldn't allow the astrologer to use astrology to justify arguing for the legitimacy of astrological reasoning. So why should the skeptic allow you to use memory in justifying your belief that it is legitimate for you to rely on memory? Without relying on memory, however, we seem to be prisoners of an all too fleeting present that simply allows no time for the kind of reasoning necessary to gain justification.

Other Skeptical Problems

Just as skeptics try to exploit the logical gap between truths about sensory experience and truths about the physical world to generate the epistemological problem of perception, and the logical gap between what we seem to remember and what actually happened to generate the epistemological problem of memory, so also, the skeptic generates a number of other famous epistemological problems by focusing on analogous gaps. So while in generating the problem of perception the skeptic might give you inductive reasoning, the legitimacy of that reasoning might itself become the target of skeptical attack. You infer from your observation of a near constant correlation between F's and G's that the next F will be a G. But what reason do you have for believing that the premises of this argument make probable the conclusion? Is it that you have successfully employed arguments of this sort in the past to generate true conclusions? But that's an argument of the type under skeptical attack, and the skeptic will insist that you not beg the question by using inductive reasoning to establish its own legitimacy. The problem of finding some non-question begging justification for accepting the legitimacy of inductive reasoning is known as the *problem of induction*.

Generating the epistemological *problem of other minds* proceeds from the relatively unproblematic observation that the only evidence we have from which we can infer the mental states of others is what we know about their physical behavior. When I conclude that you are in pain I do so by noticing that you are grimacing or that you are complaining or that you are behaving in some other way associated with pain. But what reason do I have for supposing that such behavior is correlated with pain? To be sure, if we have knowledge of the external world and knowledge of our own past, we might be able to correlate our own pain behavior with our own pain. But the skeptic will complain that we are guilty of hasty generalization if we attempt to infer a general correlation between this sort of behavior and pain from our observation of the correlation of those properties in a single person.

Setting aside skeptical problems concerning the physical world, the future, the past, and other minds, philosophers of science find themselves wondering how the theoretical physicist can reach justified conclusions about the world of so-called theoretical entities, entities like quarks that are sometimes thought of us as unobservable in principle. It is trivially true that one cannot observe a correlation between that which can be observed and that which by its nature cannot be observed. Induction seems hopeless as a route to knowledge of the unobservable. As we saw earlier, it is not easy to find a plausible argument to the best explanation that does not itself collapse into inductive reasoning.

Externalist Responses to the Skeptic

Noninferential justification

As we saw in the last chapter, part of the attraction externalism holds for many epistemologists is the ease with which the view can deflect skeptical arguments. As we also saw, that very power leaves others worried about whether the externalist has captured a philosophically interesting concept of justification – a concept the satisfaction of which satisfies philosophical curiosity. But let us begin by looking at how the externalist might approach the classic skeptical arguments. And let us again take as our example skepticism with respect to the external world.

The skeptic, you will recall, claimed that in certain skeptical scenarios (dreams, hallucinations, and the like) we possess the same justification for believing what we do about our physical environment that we would were our experience veridical. The skeptic then argued that if that is so then the justification we possess in the veridical case must not be noninferential for it can't consist in some sort of direct acquaintance with the truth maker for what we believe. If we think back to some of the externalist accounts of noninferential justification that we considered in chapter 5, we will see that there are two quite different responses to the argument. On one externalist account of noninferential justification, a belief that P is noninferentially justified when it is caused by the fact that P, where the causal chain involves no intermediate belief links. On such an account of noninferential justification, it makes perfectly good sense to suppose that in the veridical case (the case where the red object is, by hypothesis, causally responsible for both my visual experience and the belief that experience produces) my belief that the physical object exists is noninferentially justified. In the nonveridical case, the belief, by hypothesis, is produced by some fact other than the truth maker for what is believed and thus is not noninferentially justified. We are, given the view, ideally positioned to challenge the skeptic's claim that in veridical and nonveridical perception we can possess the very same sort of justification for believing what we do about our immediate physical surroundings.

The causal theory, however, was just one account of noninferential justification. The reliabilist, you will recall, suggested that we might have a noninferentially justified belief that there exists some physical object before us that is red and round provided that there is some belief-independent, unconditionally reliable belief-forming process that results in my believing that the red, round object exists. The reliabilist can concede that the justification I possess in both veridical and nonveridical situations is the same (the fact that the belief results from the right sort of reliable process), but deny that that implies that in the veridical case the belief is not noninferentially justified. If noninferential justification involved some direct relation between a believer and the truth condition for what is believed, it would follow that if the justification I possess in the veridical case is the same as the justification I possess in the nonveridical case then I don't possess noninferential justification in the veridical case. But as we saw, reliabilism divorces the concept of noninferential justification entirely from the concept of infallible belief. Indeed, according to the reliabilist, a noninferentially justified belief might be barely more likely to be true than false. All that is required for a belief to be noninferentially justified is that it result from a process that takes as its inputs no belief states and is unconditionally reliable – results in true beliefs more often than not. To be sure, there is a real question about whether the belief-forming process that results in belief in the veridical case is the same as the belief-forming process that results in belief in the skeptical scenarios. We discussed the problem of generality in chapter 5. But it wouldn't be that hard for the reliabilist to come up with a characterization of visual belief-forming processes that allows that the same process (one that takes as its input something like visual sensation) operates in both the veridical and the hallucinatory case. If the process is the same and if we are rarely in skepical scenarios then we might very well have noninferentially justified beliefs about our physical environment in both veridical and nonveridical situations.

Inferential justification

Just as the externalist allows for the possibility of a dramatically broader foundation upon which to build justified belief, so also the externalist's standards for inferential justification are far more lenient than those of the inferential internalists. As you will recall, virtually all externalists allow that one can be inferentially justified in believing some proposition provided that the right connection obtains between "input" beliefs and "output" beliefs. To acquire inferential justification there is no requirement that the believer be aware of the appropriate inferential connections. It is enough that the connections obtain. So, for example, on a crude causal theory, if my belief that P is caused (in the right way) directly by the fact that P (without any beliefs constituting mediate links in a causal chain) then my belief that P will be noninferentially justified. And if my belief that Q is caused by the fact that Q but via a causal chain that involves other justified beliefs, my belief that Q will be inferentially justified.

On a reliabilist's view, any causal connection between beliefs might yield inferential justification provided that the "input" beliefs are justified and the "output" beliefs are produced by a conditionally reliable process (one that would yield true belief most of the time when the input beliefs are true). If I believe that I'm going to have a bad day because I believe that a black cat walked before me, the former belief might be inferentially justified. It might be the case that, to most people's surprise, black cats have all sorts of powers to influence the destiny of human beings and exercise those powers on most occasions when they cross the paths of human beings.

It's also an interesting feature of most externalisms that there should be no objection in principle to using a way of forming beliefs to acquire a justified belief that that way of forming belief is justified. Consider again reliabilism. We want to know whether or not reliance on memory is a good way to arrive at truths about the past. Traditional epistemologists consider the following argument a non-starter:

1   I seem to remember seeming to remember doing a great many things and I further seem to remember that most of the time I seem to remember doing those things I actually did those things.

Therefore,

2   Relying on memory usually allows one to arrive at the truth.

The skeptic will charge you with an almost pathetic circularity. You cannot use memory to acquire justified belief that memory is legitimate. But if reliabilism is true, and if memory is a reliable belief-forming process and induction (generalization from past experience) is a reliable belief-forming process then one can, according to the view, get oneself justified belief in the reliability of memory in precisely this way. Furthermore, one can get oneself justified belief in the reliability of perception by relying on memory, perception and induction (assuming again that these ways of producing beliefs are in fact reliable).

I have argued elsewhere that the ease with which most externalisms allow one to acquire justified belief that one has justified belief (in more technical language, *metajustification*) might be taken as a kind of *reductio ad absurdum* of the view.[3] And it is interesting to note that even many externalists seem to get cold feet when they contemplate the prospects of employing their reliable belief-forming processes to acquire justified belief that those processes are reliable. But I think in the end the objection is no stronger than one we have already had occasion to note. While we may have all sorts of noninferentially and inferentially justified beliefs on externalist analyses of justification, should we be fortunate enough to live in a world in which those beliefs are produced in the right way, it hardly seems that this does an intellectually curious person a whole lot of good when it comes to satisfying that intellectual curiosity. As the infamous newspaper suggests, inquiring minds want to know. But they want to know in a way that provides *assurance* that what they believe is true.

Internalist Responses to the Skeptic

It seems to me that the popularity of externalism in epistemology is a direct consequence of the difficulties the internalist faces in trying to meet the skeptic's challenge. Indeed, when Quine in "Epistemology Naturalized" first urged us to naturalize epistemology – to study knowledge presupposing the legitimacy of scientific methods and the conclusions reached employing those methods – he justified his suggestion in large part by pointing to the singular lack of success that traditional foundationalists had trying to justify the conclusions of "common sense" from the meager premises allowed by infallible justification or justification provided by direct acquaintance with facts.[4] In fact, I do think that the traditional (internalist) foundationalist has an uphill battle responding to the skeptic.

We looked at a number of specific skeptical arguments in an effort to uncover the structure of those arguments and the presuppositions, usually internalist presuppositions, that the skeptic relied on in presenting those arguments. Let's re-examine what is in many ways the most fundamental of those skeptical arguments, the argument questioning the justification we have for believing propositions about the past based on memory.

The skeptic grants us that we may seem to remember having had a certain experience – say, having had a headache this morning. The skeptic wants to know, however, how we found out that seeming to remember having a headache is a reliable indicator of actually having had one. In taking that question to be critical, the skeptic is presupposing inferential internalism. Without some reason for thinking that the available evidence (in this case the apparent memory) makes our conclusion likely (the claim about an earlier experience), we have no reason to believe our conclusion based on our evidence. But, the skeptic argued, we cannot rely on memory in answering the challenge without begging the question. We cannot, for example, point out that we seem to remember many occasions on which we seemed to remember things that actually occurred.

In fact, I suspect, the traditional foundationalist's only hope is to argue for an interpretation of the relation of making probable common sense takes to hold between premises and conclusion that makes that relation knowable without inference – that makes that relation, in effect, more like entailment. Consider a deductively valid argument (and remember Carroll's dialogue between the Tortoise and Achilles). I infer Q from my knowledge of P and (if P then Q). The skeptic wants to know what reason I have for believing that (P and if P then Q) entails Q. I would, of course, fall into the skeptic's trap if I try to answer the question employing yet another *argument*. That argument will have premises and a conclusion, and I will inevitably need reason for believing that those premises bear the right relation to that conclusion. We avoid the skeptic's trap, however, by claiming that we can often know without inference that entailment relations hold between propositions. On an acquaintance theory, for example, I might claim to be directly acquainted with the relation of entailment holding between the bearers of truth value (perhaps thoughts). Entailment is, arguably, the upper limit of making probable. Perhaps, I can also convince myself that I sometimes know without inference when one proposition makes probable another.

In chapter 6, we examined the Keynesian view of probability relations in the context of our discussion of inferential internalism. It is precisely that relation that could play a critical role in allowing the traditional foundationalist to avoid a fairly radical skepticism. If we can convince ourselves that when we seem to see a table that makes prima facie probable that there is a table there, that when we seem to remember having had a headache this morning that makes it *prima facie* probable that we did have a headache this morning, that when we have observed an impressive correlation between two phenomena X and Y with no observations of an X without a Y, that makes it *prima facie* probable that the next X will be a Y, then we have a fighting chance to respond to the skeptic's challenge. The key move in the response is to refuse the invitation to answer the skeptic with another argument designed to establish the connection between our evidence and our conclusions. The key is to argue for a relation of making probable that can hold between propositions where we can at least sometimes know that without inference it holds.

The argument for the existence of such a relation is in a way no more, but also no less, plausible than arguments we have already discussed against various versions of externalism. The reliabilist, you will recall, was criticized by some for holding that the victims of demonic machination had unjustified beliefs about their surroundings. The beliefs were, to be sure, unreliably produced. The vast majority of such beliefs were false. But there is a strong intuition many share that if one had precisely the same sensory evidence in a demonic environment as we have in ours, one would have precisely the same justification for believing various and sundry truths about one's physical environment. What this might seem to show

134

is that there are necessary truths about what makes probable what – necessary truths knowable *a priori*. And that is precisely what the Keynesian is arguing.

Conclusion

We have seen that one's response to the skeptic, indeed, the way in which one approaches any applied epistemological inquiry, depends critically on the set of metaepistemological assumptions one brings to the table. On most versions of epistemic externalism, it requires only that the world cooperate in various ways for us to gain all sorts of knowledge and epistemic justification. The epistemic internalist is convinced that the epistemic reward of epistemic assurance – the satisfaction of epistemic curiosity – requires the honest but demanding toil of discovering appropriate connections between one's evidence and one's conclusion. The price of setting such high standards for knowledge and justification is that one might never achieve one's epistemic goals.

Suggested readings

Ayer, A. J. 1956. *The Problem of Knowledge*, chapter 2. Edinburgh: Penguin.
Conee, Earl and Feldman, Richard. 2004. "Making Sense of Skepticism." In *Evidentialism*. Oxford: Oxford University Press.
Huemer, Mike. 2001. *Skepticism and the Veil of Perception*, chapter 2. Lanham, MD: Rowman and Littlefield.
Hume, David. 1888. *A Treatise of Human Nature*, ed. L. A. Selby-Bigge, book I, part IV, sec. 2. London: Oxford University Press.

Notes

1 An analogy is often used to help explain the view. When we say that John danced a jig, we might take the grammar of our sentence to suggest that there is this activity, the jig, upon which John performed the act of dancing. But a bit of reflection suggests that the jig John danced is just John's dancing a certain way.

2 Indeed, when you think about it, the prevalence of flood myths in ancient cultures is surely caused in part by the fact that ancient people must have been genuinely puzzled about the remains of what were clearly sea creatures embedded in rocks found in areas far removed from existing water. One natural

explanation of how water could have been in a place not usually covered by water is flooding.

3 For another attempt to develop this criticism see Stewart Cohen (2002).

4 In a similar spirit, Goldman (1999) also argues that if the internalist restricts the conditions that can justify to internal states there won't be the resources to justify most of what we commonsensically take to know and justifiably believe. For a response to Goldman see Conee and Feldman (2001).

Bibliography

Alston, William. 1989. "An Internalist Externalism." In *Epistemic Justification*. Ithaca: Cornell University Press.

Alston, William and Brandt, Richard. 1967. *The Problems of Philosophy*. Boston: Allyn and Bacon.

Armstrong. David. 1973. *Belief, Truth and Knowledge*. London: Cambridge University Press.

Audi, Robert. 1998. *Epistemology*, Introduction. New York and London: Routledge.

Ayer, A. J. 1956. *The Problem of Knowledge*, chapter 2. Edinburgh: Penguin.

Berkeley, George. 1954. *Three Dialogues Between Hylas and Philonous*. Colin M. Turbayne, ed. Indianapolis: Bobbs-Merrill.

BonJour, Laurence. 1985. *The Structure of Empirical Knowledge*. Cambridge, MA: Harvard University Press.

Bonjour, Laurence and Sosa, Ernest. 2003. *Epistemic Justification*. Oxford: Blackwell.

Butchvarov, Panayot. 1970. *The Concept of Knowledge*. Evanston, IL: Northwestern University Press.

Carroll, Lewis. 1895. "What the Tortoise Said to Achilles." *Mind*, 4, 278–80.

Chisholm, R. M. 1966. *Theory of Knowledge*, 1st edn. Englewood Cliffs, NJ: Prentice-Hall.

Cohen, Stewart. 1999. "Contextualism, Skepticism, and the Structure of Reasons." *Philosophical Perspectives*, 13, 57–89.

——. 2002. "Basic Knowledge and the Problem of Easy Knowledge." *Philosophy and Phenomenological Research*, 65, 309–29.

Conee, Earl and Feldman, Richard. 1998. "The Generality Problem for Reliabilism." *Philosophical Studies*, 89, 1–29.

——. 2001. "Internalism Defended." In *Epistemology: Internalism and Externalism*. Hilary Kornblith, ed. Oxford: Blackwell.

137

Conee, Earl and Feldman, Richard. 2004. "Making Sense of Skepticism." In *Evidentialism*. Oxford: Oxford University Press.

DePaul, Michael, ed., 2001. *Resurrecting Old-Fashioned Foundationalism*. Lanham, MD: Rowman and Littlefield.

Fales, Evan. 1996. *A Defense of the Given*, chapters 1 and 6. Lanham, MD: Rowman and Littlefield.

Fantl, Jeremy and Matthew McGrath. 2002. "Evidence, Pragmatics and Justification." *Philosophical Review*, 111, 67–94.

Feldman, Richard. 2001. "We Are All Naturalists Now." APA Paper Presentation.

Foley, Richard. 1979. "Justified Inconsistent Beliefs." *American Philosophical Quarterly*, 16, 247–58.

——. 1987. *The Theory of Epistemic Rationality*. Cambridge, MA: Harvard University Press.

Fumerton, Richard. 1989. "Russelling Causal Theories of Reference." In *Rereading Russell*. Wade Savage and C. Anthony Anderson, eds. Minneapolis: University of Minnesota Press.

——. 1996. *Metaepistemology and Skepticism*. Lanham, MD: Rowman and Littlefield.

——. 2002. *Realism and the Correspondence Theory of Truth*. Lanham, MD: Rowman and Littlefield.

Gettier, Edmund. 1963. "Is Justified True Belief Knowledge?" *Analysis*, 23, 121–3.

Ginet, Carl. 1988. "The Fourth Condition." In David M. Austin, ed., *Philosophical Analysis*. Dordrecht; Boston: Kluwer Academic Publishers.

Goldman, Alvin. 1967. "A Causal Theory of Knowing." *Journal of Philosophy*, 64, 355–72.

——. 1979. "What Is Justified Belief?" In *Justification and Knowledge*. George Pappas, ed. Dordrecht: Reidel, pp. 1–23.

——. 1986. *Epistemology and Cognition*. Cambridge, MA: Harvard University Press.

——. 1988. "Strong and Weak Justification." In James Toberlin, ed., *Philosophical Perspectives 2: Epistemology*. Atascadero: Ridgeview Publishing Co., pp. 51–69.

——. 1999. "Internalism Exposed." *Journal of Philosophy*, 96, 271–93.

Haack, Susan. 1995. *Evidence and Inquiry: Towards Reconstruction in Epistemology*. Cambridge: Blackwell Publishers.

Hawthorne, John. 2003. *Knowledge and Lotteries*. Oxford: Clarendon Press.

Huemer, Mike. 2001. *Skepticism and the Veil of Perception*. Lanham, MD: Rowman and Littlefield.

——. 2002. "Fumerton's Principle of Inferential Justification." *Journal of Philosophical Research*, 27, 329–40.

Hume, David. 1888. *A Treatise of Human Nature*. L. A. Selby-Bigge, ed. London: Oxford University Press.

Keynes, John. 1921. *A Treatise on Probability*. London: Macmillan.

Bibliography

Klein, Peter. 1998. "Foundationalism and the Infinite Regress of Reasons." *Philosophy and Phenomenological Research*, 58 (4), 919–25.

——. 1999. "Human Knowledge and the Infinite Regress of Reasons." *Philosophical Perspectives*, 13, 297–325.

Kripke, Saul. 1980. *Naming and Necessity*. Cambridge, MA: Harvard University Press.

Lehrer, Keith. 1974. *Knowledge*. Oxford: Oxford University Press.

Lewis, David. 1996. "Elusive Knowledge." *Australasian Journal of Philosophy*, 5, 49–67.

McGrew, Timothy, 1995. *The Foundations of Knowledge*. Lanham, MD: Littlefield Addams.

Nozick, Robert. 1981. *Philosophical Explanations*. Cambridge, MA: Harvard University Press.

Peirce, C. S. 1938. *Collected Papers*. C. Hartshorne and P. Weis, eds. Cambridge, MA: Harvard University Press.

Plantinga, Alvan. 1992. "Justification in the 20th Century." In *Philosophical Issues 2: Rationality in Epistemology*. Enrique Villanueva, ed. Atascadero, CA: Ridgeview Publishing Co., pp. 43–78.

——. 1993. *Warrant and Proper Function*. New York: Oxford University Press.

——. 2000. *Warranted Christian Belief*. New York: Oxford University Press.

Quine, W. V. O. 1969. "Epistemology Naturalized." In *Ontological Relativity and Other Essays*. New York: Columbia University Press.

Russell, Bertrand. 1948. *Human Knowledge: Its Scope and Limits*. New York: Simon and Schuster.

——. 1959. *The Problems of Philosophy*. Oxford: Oxford University Press.

Sellars, Wilfred. 1963. *Science, Perception and Reality*. London: Routledge and Kegan Paul.

Sosa, Ernest. 1991. *Knowledge in Perspective*. Cambridge: Cambridge University Press.

Stanley, Jason. 2003. "Context, Interest–Relativity and Knowledge." Unpublished. University of Michigan.

Williamson, Timothy. 2000. *Knowledge and its Limits*. Oxford University Press.

Wilson, Jennifer. 2004. "Rethinking the *A Priori/A Posteriori* Distinction." Unpublished. University of Iowa.

Index

Note: "n." after a page number indicates the number of a note on that page.